GUIDE'S GREATEST STORIES

GUIDE'S GREATEST STORIES

Compiled
by Randy Fishell

REVIEW AND HERALD® PUBLISHING ASSOCIATION
HAGERSTOWN, MD 21740

This book was
Edited by Gerald Wheeler
Designed by Patricia S. Wegh
Cover design by Bill Kirstein
Illustrations by Terry Crews
Typeset: 12/13.5 Clearface

PRINTED IN U.S.A.

98 97 96 95 94   10 9 8 7 6 5 4 3 2 1

R&H Cataloging Service
Guide's greatest stories. Compiled by
    Randy Fishell.

    1. Short stories—Collections.   I. Fishell,
Randy, comp.   II. Guide magazine.

        808.8

ISBN 0-8280-0891-4

A note to authors: In putting this book together, we did our best to con-
tact each of you. If your story appears here and we were unable to reach
you, please write to us at Guide, 55 West Oak Ridge Drive, Hagerstown,
MD 21740. Thanks!

CONTENTS

AMAZING ENDINGS

INCREDIBLE ADVENTURES

LIFECHANGING DISCOVERIES

Narrow Escapes

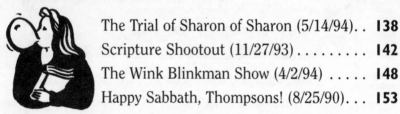

Parables 'n' Stuff

ACKNOWLEDGMENTS

A special thanks to the previous editors of *Guide*.® Their suggestions regarding great stories from the past helped immensely in putting this book together. Also, thanks to Michelle Sturm and Kerri Brown for their part in getting yesteryear's stories onto today's computers.

GUIDE
EDITORIAL STAFF
· ·

EDITORS
Lawrence Maxwell, 1952-70

Lowell Litten, 1970-83

Penny Estes Wheeler, 1983-86

Jeannette Johnson, 1986-present

ASSOCIATE EDITOR
Randy Fishell, 1993-present

ASSISTANT EDITORS
Jan Wuerstlin, 1977-84

Jeannette Johnson, 1983-86

Suzanne Perdew, 1986-89

Randy Fishell, 1989-93

CAN YOU *BELIEVE* IT?

An escaped convict shows up for supper. An *angel* repairs a bicycle tire. A soldier rescues *75* men while bullets hit inches away.

It's true: there are lots of amazing, incredible, lifechanging stories in this book. And maybe you're thinking, *Why doesn't that astonishing-type stuff ever happen to me?*

Well . . .

- Your heart beats in perfect rhythm day after day. *AMAZING!*

- At school, you whiz through a much-feared quiz. *INCREDIBLE!*

- A cosmic King dies for *you* on a criminal's cross. *LIFECHANGING,* to say the least.

Each day is jam-packed with *grace*—and miracles large and small.

Maybe someday you'll find yourself involved in a dramatic episode similar to one of these *Guide*® stories. Or maybe you won't. No matter. Just keep your heart in touch with heaven, and your life will become one of *God's* greatest stories.

Randy Fishell

AMAZING
ENDINGS

1

OUT OF THE BLUE

by John F. Jessel

MOM SWUNG HARD, but the ball dropped behind her. "Hoo-eee!" I yelled. "The breeze from that one cooled me off way out here in the outfield."

From the pitcher's mound Dad said, "Great cut, dear. If you'd have connected, that ball would've sailed into orbit."

She laughed. "All I want to do is send another high fly over John's head. He needs more dance practice." She was teasing me about an earlier hit. Backpedaling to catch it, I'd jostled our birdbath. Some ballerina-like moves saved the seat of my pants from grass stains and my shirt from a soggy feather shower. Who said backyard whiffle ball was safer than bungee jumping?

While Mom bent to retrieve the ball, I fixed my cap to shade my eyes. The late-afternoon sun had slipped lower, so seeing a ball hit toward me was getting hard. I didn't mind much. "The sun was in my eyes" was always a good reason for missing pop-ups. And sometimes it was even true.

I glanced back at Mom. She'd picked up the ball, but she hadn't tossed it to Dad. She just stood there, frozen—like a statue. Before I realized that something was wrong, she dropped the ball and bat, threw her hands to her cheeks, and screamed.

Dad scrambled toward her. "Honey! What? What?" he yelled, his voice scratchier and higher than I'd ever heard it before.

Then I was running too, so fast that my cap flew off. *She's sick,* I thought. Stories of sudden death from natural causes filled my head. Choking. Heart attacks. Strokes. Fear squeezed my chest.

Dad reached her just before I did. She'd now fallen to her knees, and I hoped that was a good sign. Still, her face was pale and her breath came in deep gasps.

"Tell me! Tell me!" my father shouted, trying to pry her hands from her cheeks.

His urgency seemed to take effect. She slid one hand to her throat and pointed over our shoulders with the other. "Look!" she rasped. "It's crashing!"

"It? What?" Dad spun around to look behind him. "Oh, no, *no!*"

I turned and looked. Two men were floating to earth beneath their parachutes. They looked small, almost toylike in the distance. And then I noticed a third shape in the sky—a thing growing larger by the second.

"It's their plane," Mom said. "They've bailed out . . . It's crashing!"

I looked at Dad, half expecting him to burst into laughter and tell her that they were skydivers, and the plane heading our way was his buddy Art's. Art loved to fly low over our house and dip a wing as a hello to Dad.

I looked back at the plane. It was much closer now, and much lower, streaking toward us like a bullet. What I heard was not the buzz of a Piper Cub but the shriek of a jet. It looked like a shiny-scaled bird of prey, hunting anything stupid enough to stand in its path.

Dad grabbed me by the shoulder and Mom around the waist. "Let's run!" I screeched over the howl of engines that were roaring like hurricane winds.

"We can't beat it," Dad yelled. "*Just get down!*" He pushed me to my knees, hard, then to my stomach. He brought Mom down too, then fell between us. "Put your arms over your head!"

I already had.

In seconds the jet's noise doubled, then doubled again. The thing was nearly upon us. My heart fluttered like a trapped butterfly; I was too scared to find words to pray. "Jesus . . . Dear Jesus" was all I could muster. And then the jet's roar built to what seemed like a thousand hurricanes. Suddenly I couldn't overcome my desire to face the beast. I looked up.

I wasn't the only one staring toward the roar of death. Both Mom and Dad had focused on the sleek-winged monster streaking so close to our backyard maple that twigs shook and leaves fell in its slipstream. Glittering metal and a perfectly white star inside a circle of blue flashed over us in ear-numbing, bone-rattling noise. And then I was looking into the jet's black exhaust ports.

"It missed us, Dad!" I shouted in elation.

Mom's voice brought me back to reality. "But it's heading toward the school, son! Pray for them!"

She meant the band. We'd heard them in after-school marching practice while we'd played ball. They'd have little chance to escape the screaming monster descending from the blue.

Again my mind numbed. But Mom's voice sounded strong against the softening jet roar. "Please, Lord, let it miss the school. Please let it fall where it will harm no one."

Two seconds after Mom's prayer the jet's nose turned skyward. The plane seemed almost to stand on its tail in a steep climb. My mouth dropped.

"Autopilot," Dad said as a new roar hit our ears.

"Please, God, please," Mom repeated.

Now the jet broke its climb, then dipped sharply earthward. No sound came from its engines. The sudden quiet seemed more terrible than the earlier roar.

"It stalled," Dad said. "Now it'll drop like a stone."

The jet plummeted behind a grove of trees, and for a second I thought I'd dreamed everything. Then a thunderclap and a cloud of black smoke rising from behind the tree line told me my nightmare was far too real.

Mom turned to Dad, her eyes questioning, fearful. He bit his lip and shook his head. She closed her eyes and prayed aloud, "Help them, Lord."

The wail of sirens filled the late-evening air as emergency vehicles from all across town sped to the crash site. Our kitchen echoed with neighbors jabbering excitedly about their actions as the jet roared into and out of our lives. Like Mom, many had prayed for their deliverance and the safety of others. Even now some prayed aloud for people at the crash site.

Dad's radio blared updates on the crash. By nightfall a newscast grew specific. The jet had missed the school, but a small grocery store had been hit. Its cement block walls lay in rubble. A few shoppers had escaped unhurt; others were feared trapped. Quiet descended upon the kitchen as our neighbors fell into whispered prayers. I soon drifted asleep to the sound of the news anchor's voice.

The next morning the first thing I heard when I woke up was the sound of a radio interview with the pilot.

"I put it on autopilot, then ejected," he was saying. "The bird should have banked away, but it headed toward the town. I don't know why . . . But then neither do I know how it dropped into a city without causing any injuries."

For a second I thought the newscaster would correct the mistake. No injuries? But the pilot went on, uninterrupted. Was it true?

The pilot said, "All I thought about on my way down was that we needed a miracle. Well, one came, though I'm not sure how."

I grinned when I heard that. I thought about Mom's first prayer and the plane's last-second acrobatics. I thought about my neighbors telling about similar prayers, and of hearing still more prayers in our kitchen that night. And then I thought, *Yep, we got a miracle. But, Mr. Pilot, I think I have an idea how it came about.*

JUST BY A THREAD

by Keith Knoche

GLADYS AND LOTTIE were excited! This was the weekend of the revival at the Monte Vista church. Pastor Thurlow had announced that a visiting minister from Philadelphia was going to be speaking on Bible prophecy and the end of the world. Gladys was looking forward to seeing her friends and listening to the good gospel music. Lottie liked the preaching, but especially enjoyed the wide variety of delicious food at the potluck.

The hours of that day moved on at a snail's pace. Both girls were eager for sunset and the meeting scheduled for 7:30.

Bessie Wright was a stern mother. She would tolerate no monkey business from her girls and had given specific instructions that they were to be washed and dressed, ready to ride to town no later than 6:30. Neither of the girls needed coaxing this time.

In fact, Gladys and Lottie were dressed and ready by 4:00. Both were clean and crisp in their white dresses with full skirts to the ankle.

At 13, Gladys was more mature. She decided to pass the time by reading a book. So she sat on the front porch and was soon engrossed in her story.

Lottie was only 9 and not so easily entertained. She busied herself throwing a ball against the side of the house. That seemed to satisfy her until the ball took an unexpected bounce off the wall and sailed over a nearby barbed-wire fence.

No problem. She would simply fetch the ball back. She maneuvered her way through the fence, got the ball, and was attempting to return when a terrible thing happened. Her beautiful white dress caught on the sharp wire and ripped—a huge triangle-shaped tear slashed into the soft, white fabric. Lottie began to cry.

Gladys put down her book when she heard crying around the corner of the house. She quickly ran to her teary-eyed sister and tried to comfort her.

"Now I won't be able to go to the meeting at the church," Lottie sobbed. "I don't have another dress, and this one is ruined!"

"It's OK, Lottie," Gladys answered. "Let's go see if Mom can fix it."

The girls made their way into the house and explained the problem. Mother was upset. It was nearly sundown, and there was simply no time to mend the torn dress. And Lottie had no other Sabbath dress. She would have to stay home and miss the revival.

Gladys tried to pin the tear with a safety pin. But it didn't work. The rip was too big and too obvious.

There were tears in Lottie's eyes as she watched the rest of the family head for town and the revival meeting. She had to stay home with her aunt and miss the good times. But then, she had only herself to blame.

There was an obvious vacancy in the church pew next to Gladys. Lottie always sat right beside her for prayer meeting and church service. Gladys felt bad that her sister was absent as the weekend revival began. But when it came time for prayer, she knelt and included a new sentence in her petition to God. "Lord, please mend Lottie's dress so that she can come to church tomorrow."

It was a simple request, uttered in childlike faith. Perhaps fixing her sister's Sabbath dress was too small a thing to ask of a big God. After all, God was probably only concerned about the big problems—like keeping planets in their courses or helping control the weather. Nevertheless, Gladys prayed that the tear in the dress would be mended.

Morning dawned bright and clear. It was Sabbath, and there would be meetings at the church—family, friends, fun, and food. Gladys bounded from bed and hurried into Lottie's room to check the closet.

Lottie was rubbing sleep from her eyes. She had been totally unaware of her sister's prayer. "What are you doing in my closet?" she protested.

"I want to see your Sabbath dress," Gladys responded.

"You know I tore that dress and will have to stay home from church again today," Lottie said sadly.

Gladys paid no attention and rummaged through the hanging clothes until she found the dress. Pulling it out, she threw it across the bed to search for the tear.

"Lottie, the tear is gone!" Gladys gasped. Both girls scanned the entire dress, every square inch, but could find no trace of the tear. It was as though the dress had never been torn at all.

Lottie looked at her sister with round eyes. "How did my dress get fixed?" she asked.

"I don't know," Gladys responded in disbelief. "I prayed for God to mend it. I guess last night He did."

Gladys clutched the dress and ran downstairs with Lottie close behind.

"Mom! Mom!" Gladys shouted. "The dress—Lottie's dress has been fixed! The tear is gone!"

Mother was sitting on the sofa talking to her friend Mavis. "Let me see the dress. I didn't have time to repair the tear yet," she said. "You girls just didn't look carefully enough. The tear is there all right." She began to look for the rip in the garment. She looked and looked. Pretty soon Mavis joined in. Both ladies went over every inch of fabric, but the tear was gone. It had vanished. There was absolutely no sign that the Sabbath dress had ever been damaged. It was just like brand-new!

"What do you make of it?" asked Mavis.

"I don't know," Mother said quietly.

Gladys couldn't keep silent another minute. "Mom, last night at revival I prayed that God would mend Lottie's dress so she could go to church today, and God answered my prayer!"

The two women looked somewhat skeptical. Yet there was no denying the fact that the dress was like new. Maybe God was in the business of answering simple, heartfelt prayers. Maybe God could mend dresses better than the best seamstress. The white dress was proof. God does care about little things.

Lottie wore the "miracle dress" to church that Sabbath and for many Sabbaths to come. Folks all over the San Luis Valley came to see the dress, hear the story, and be amazed.

Maybe some of you are wondering if this story is really true. I can tell you for a fact that it is absolutely true! You see, these events happened back in the year 1912. Gladys is my grandmother. And last Sabbath afternoon I sat and listened as she recounted the story again. Nearly 80 years of retelling have not diminished the wonder of the night God played tailor.

No Hoofprints

by Lorabel P. Midkiff

WE'RE ALMOST THERE, old girl. It's been a long, hot day," Mr. Rubi said to the old swayback plow horse he had ridden for the past ten hours. *Clippety-clop, clippety-clop,* over the dusty road they plodded on. "Twelve hours by bus yesterday and now all day with you. We'll stop before dark, old girl."

After a good night's sleep at the house where he left the borrowed horse, Mr. Rubi started out on foot. Two and a half days over the narrow footpath that snaked up the Sierra Madre Mountains seemed like two and a half weeks to the weary traveler. "This is the hardest trip I've ever made," he sighed. "I should be getting close. I'm sure this box weighs twice what it did when I started out."

When he finally caught sight of the village, he set his box down next to his rolled-up *serape,* and sat on a rock in the shade of an ironwood tree. For a long time he looked across the gully to the little village of Galeana. He could see the church steeple, the central plaza, and the footbridge. "Is this really the place the Lord told me to come?" he asked half aloud. The thatched roofs poking through the dense trees and vines showed him that not all of the people lived close to the village. He had never been so far in the mountains. Then, before leaving his lookout, he prayed. "If this is where You want me to preach, God, I will not be afraid. I know You will stay close by."

It didn't matter that there were no hotels in the village; people gladly entertained strangers. The first night found Mr. Rubi staying with an Indian family of the Huitchole tribe. At once they wanted to know about the books that he carried in his big box. Even though they could not read Spanish, they listened carefully to every word he spoke or read to them. Soon they called in their friends, and the little house filled with people who listened to the story of Jesus' promise to take them to heaven.

At the end of the week more than 20 people met for their first Sabbath school. The second week almost 50 scrubbed-up, happy men and women crowded around the well in the backyard. What a wonderful time they had singing, praying, and repeating the verses they had memorized.

Early the following morning the religious leader of the community and one of the leader's big, strong members came to Mr. Rubi, warning, "You will leave the village by sundown tonight."

But Mr. Rubi kept right on with his work.

The next morning, the two men returned. The strong man placed his hand on Mr. Rubi's shoulder and threatened, "If you are not gone by noon today, we will kill you."

"All right," the missionary answered, "but I will have to talk to God about it first. If He wants me to leave, I will go. But if He wants me to stay and work with these good people, I cannot go."

"Good people, yes. But they are *our* people. We don't want any of your preaching here in our village. No one ever comes up here to interfere, but now everyone is talking about your new religion. Get out of town while you are still alive—or we will cut you up for buzzard food!" He wasn't joking.

"God, which do You want me to do—preach to these people or get cut up for buzzard food? If You want me to preach, I am ready; if You want me to be food for the birds, I am ready for that, too. Make it clear to me by noon today. Thank You, God." Faithfully Mr. Rubi went about the work he had come to do. Just as faithfully he kept praying that God would not permit the enemy to stop His work.

As Mr. Rubi was crossing the small footbridge at noon, two men jumped up from under the far end of the bridge and ran toward him, waving their *machetes* over their heads. "They sent us to kill you, stranger." Their devilish eyes flashed wildly, and their snarling lips spat out the order, "Give us your last word."

"Oh, you are very kind, my friends. I do have one last request." He struggled to be calm. "I want to talk to my Jesus just one more time. I would not want to die without thanking Him for giving me such a good life. He is my very best Friend, you see." The killers looked at each other stupidly, nodded, and watched as the stranger knelt down on the little bridge and began to pray.

"Here comes a man on horseback! Let's get out of here!" Mr. Rubi heard one of the men say as they scurried away. He got up from his knees and looked for the horse, which he too had heard, but it was nowhere in sight.

A man was walking toward the bridge, so Mr. Rubi asked, "Did you see the horse and rider that just went by?"

"My friend, I saw you kneeling in the middle of the bridge with two men standing over you. All of a sudden the men ran off, and you got up. But certainly no horse and rider crossed that bridge."

Mr. Rubi searched for hoofprints on the dusty road, but could not find a single one. And as he looked up and down the road he thought he heard a voice saying, "Go and preach."

GUARDIAN ANGEL

by Edna May Olsen

EACH OF US has a guardian angel, assigned to us at birth," Dad told us recently. "When we get to heaven, won't it be fun to meet them and to discover how many times they've helped and protected us in this life?" I'd heard that all my life, but somehow the reality of it struck me then.

How wonderful! I thought. *I wonder what mine looks like?* Strange to say, I believed I had met my guardian angel recently.

But—would a guardian angel wear a yellow slicker?

As I pedaled along the road in company with about 20 other kids, I wondered for the hundredth time whatever had possessed me to think I could go on a 70-mile bicycle ride. "Admit it," I told myself wearily. "You're out of shape, and it was stupid to think you could do it. Nevertheless, home is a long way off, and no one will get you there but yourself. Keep pedaling."

My back ached, as did my legs, right down to the tips of my toes. How I kept on my bike was a mystery. If I'd fallen off, I probably would have just stayed where I fell.

The ride to Baker's Point early in the morning had gone splendidly. The wind had been at our backs and we were part of it, flying along the back roads toward the sea, driven by both the wind and our enthusiasm. At last we'd clustered our bicycles together under a beach picnic shelter, secured them with chains, and sprawled gratefully out on the warm sand. A gentle offshore breeze kept us cool, although it laced our sandwiches with grit.

"But that's what a sand-wich is!" chuckled Jan, our leader, when someone complained, and we laughed uproariously. Later we waded in the ocean, gathered shells, and threw a Frisbee until he called us to order.

"I hope you haven't forgotten," he began, "but we have a long way to go, so we'd better get started. Saddle up and let's hit the road. Remember, stay together as much as possible, especially when it gets dark. Watch out for cars and stay well over on the side of the road. Ready now? Let's go."

I ached a little when I climbed back on my bicycle, but gradually the stiffness wore off and I enjoyed the ride. At first we sang, though at times it was doubtful we were singing the same song, but then we grew silent as the weariness of the journey settled in. *Home* was foremost in all our minds.

Although we stopped occasionally for drinks of water, we didn't linger, as the sun was dangerously close to the horizon.

"Are you all right?" Jan once asked, slowing down to encourage the few stragglers at the end of the column. "Keep those legs pumping and you'll be home in no time."

Then he pedaled off to the head of the procession.

The breeze of early morning had changed to a chill wind that blew directly in our faces, and we bent our heads low over the handlebars. "One, two, three, four," I counted mechanically, as tired legs drove the pedals around. "One, two, three, four."

How much farther? my legs begged my brain.

At the entrance to an abandoned farmhouse we stopped and turned on our lights.

"Only ten more miles," Jan said with a grin, "and then hot baths, a bite to eat, and soft beds."

"Ten miles," I groaned, getting back in the saddle, which by now felt like a pile of rocks. "*Only* ten more miles!"

The evening was closing in, and to add to our discomfort

it began to drizzle.

I kept my head down low, realizing to my dismay that I was falling behind. Already the leaders were out of sight, speeding toward home.

"Faster!" I urged my aching legs. "Keep up, whatever you do. If you fall behind, no one will notice."

Bang! My bicycle swerved a little, and then I recognized the *bump, bump, bump* of a flat tire.

"Oh, no," I groaned, slowing down and coming to a standstill. "A flat is the last thing I need." I glanced up in time to see the taillights of the last stragglers disappearing into the grayness.

"Well, nothing to do," I reasoned, "but to fix the tire." I fumbled for my tool kit, turned my bicycle upside down, and began to gently separate the tire from its rim.

The drizzle continued, and soon I was soaking wet. I wondered what my companions would say when they stopped again and noticed I wasn't with them. Well, no point wondering; I was on my own, and the sooner I tackled the job the better.

When the tire refused to be coaxed from the rim, hot tears of frustration mingled with perspiration and raindrops. A car flashed by, spraying me with water. I felt very alone.

Finally I straightened up and stretched my aching shoulders.

"Dear Lord," I whispered, "I'm really in a jam. Please help me."

It was then that I noticed a bobbing pinprick of light coming toward me. It was just one light so it must be, yes, it was a bicycle. Someone was coming back to help me.

"Hi," called a cheerful voice. "I missed you, and figured you had trouble of some kind. Aha, a flat, and in this weather and miles from anywhere. How did you manage that?"

My new friend gave a giggle. "First, though, you're soaked. Put this across your shoulders. It will help you a little." She draped a cape over my back. "Now, let me give you a hand. I can't think of how many of these I've fixed in my time."

My guardian angel in a yellow slicker?

Working together, we pried the tire from its rim, patched it, and replaced it.

"I hope that holds until you get home," she said, poking damp hair under her hood. "Let's put air in it and then you'll be all set."

"Wow, thanks for coming back," I said gratefully. "I couldn't have changed it alone, that's pretty obvious. But I don't remember seeing you before."

"Really?" she said lightly. "Well, I've seen *you* before. But come on now, this isn't the best place for a friendly tête-à-tête." We cycled on in silence, our tires swishing on the wet road, past the low salt marshes, Brinson's woods, and on to the first row of houses on the edge of town.

"This is where I leave you," my companion said, pointing with a wet hand to a turn in the road. "You have to continue straight until you come to Major's Corner, past the Shell station, then make a left. Take care now. See you later." And she sped away into the darkness.

"But your cape!" I called after her. The wind flung my words away, and she didn't look back.

I looked for her everywhere for weeks. I asked my friends about her, but no one had any idea who she might be.

"Perhaps she was your guardian angel," Dad said, when I recalled the incident much later.

Maybe she was, I thought in wonderment. But—a guardian angel in a yellow slicker?

OVER THE EDGE

by Hurl Bates

LIVING BACK IN these Kentucky mountains is where I want to be. Until 1977 I was in the Army, stationed in Germany for four years. Then I came down on orders for stateside and got out. Since then I've been my own boss, just sort of taking life easy.

This morning I strap my pack on my back—it weighs about 60 pounds and holds enough provisions to last a week or longer. But so far, I've never had to rely on my pack for that long.

I head north toward the Big Pine Mountains. It'll take the better part of the day to reach the summit, but I never get in any kind of hurry. I'm traveling with two of my best friends—Old Jake and Ike, my two dogs.

Last night's snow has turned the world from a dirty brown to a sort of winter wonderland. I thank God for letting me be born in a place like this where a man can live life to the full. I top the first ridge. Dawn is still about an hour away, but I can see well enough to spot deer tracks going over toward the valley that I must go through. I slip my thermos out of my pack and watch Jake and Ike warm up a trail across the valley. Old Jake is in the lead, baying excitedly. The steam from my cup curls like smoke in this cold morning air.

Slowly I rise from a crouched position and adjust my backpack, then head toward the ridge. The going is just a little slippery. Grabbing hold of a little sapling, I ease my frame over a small embankment to where a pretty good stream usually is. But today I find it frozen solid and easily walk across it.

By 9:00 a light snow starts to fall. I stand on a high rise of ground overlooking a large stretch of flat bottomland. There are no signs of the trail at all because of the snow. But I've traveled this part of the country so much I won't need any landmarks. I walk about halfway down the hill, and I notice something: it's beginning to snow more heavily.

After making my way across the rough terrain, I follow a little stream for maybe a mile. I surprise some beavers on the side of the stream bank, then make my way around the bend to a location where three mountains come together, forming a sort of flat cove. I stop here and build a fire to warm up some stew and rest. The snow has let up; it's also getting colder. I bring out my New Testament and read a couple chapters. I always feel better after reading the Good Book.

I break camp and head up the right fork of the little hollow. Near the top, I angle up the right side of the hill, knowing that when I get to the other side of this mountain it will be turning dark.

Near the top of the hill a large boulder has slid into my path, blocking the little trail. As I start to go around it, I notice there's a steep overhang just to the right of where I'm walking. I begin a sharp right turn around the boulder and grab a little sapling to steady myself. The next thing I know, I'm holding the sapling in my hand, roots and all. I lose my footing and begin sliding, facefirst, over the steep embankment. There's nothing I can do about it. I feel the rocks tear into my face and chest. I try to stop my fall, but end up doing a flip, stopping when I hit a large tree.

No one has to tell me that I'm hurt bad. I'm bleeding profusely from my face; I think my jaw is broken. I start to sit up. That's when the pain really sets in, like someone is pushing a red-hot iron into the lower part of my back. I can't move my legs. I can't even feel them.

I won't last long, bleeding like this. I've got to get it stopped before I pass out. I've got to hold onto my body heat or I'm a goner. "Please, God, is this the way I'm supposed to go? If it isn't, I'm going to need Your help."

The pain pounds through my brain like thunderbolts in a bad storm. I better get myself to a level area. Straining, I see my backpack about halfway up the hill. I have to get to it, get my sleeping bag. This cold is really taking its toll on me now. "Father, if it be Thy will, don't let me die like this."

* * *

My brother Josh and I have always been real close. This morning I'm on his mind real heavy. It came on him right out of the blue—something was wrong.

Josh had been working all morning on his wife's car, stopping only for lunch. "Honey," Josh says, "did you talk to Hurl this morning?"

She looks up. "He's not home, remember? He's up in the mountains. You talked about that yesterday."

"I know," Josh says, "but I thought he might not have gone, with this snowstorm coming in the way it has."

"You know Hurl," she grins. "He doesn't pay attention to the weather when there's something to do."

Josh pushes back from the table. "I think I'll just go and have a look around his place. I have a bad feeling about this. Probably nothing to it, but I couldn't stand it if something happened to him."

His wife says nothing, just packs him a thermos of hot chocolate.

The snow is coming down in waves. The eight-mile trip takes better than 35 minutes. Worst storm of the winter, Josh thinks. He lets himself into the house and calls my name. He already knows he won't get an answer—he can't shake the feeling. He picks up the phone and dials the emergency number. When the operator comes on the line, Josh explains the situation and asks her to help him find his brother.

"We don't usually respond unless we know there's a verified situation," she says.

"Lady, I know you get a lot of crackpot calls," Josh pleads, "but this isn't one of them. I know my brother is out there and hurt bad."

Something in his voice makes Sadie Watkins do something that's against every procedure in the book. "All our drivers are out on emergency runs right now," she says, "but I'll tell you what I can do. We have one snowmobile here. You're welcome to use it." She says she's truly sorry not to be able to do more, but there's a severe weather warning out and emergencies are keeping the entire staff busy.

Josh pushes his truck hard the four miles into town, unable to push back the desperate need to hurry.

* * *

My bleeding has slowed somewhat. I wonder if I'm bled out. I begin to feel faint. It's been dark about an hour. I keep telling myself I've got to get to my backpack.

At last my dogs have found me. I pull them close to help me stay warm. I'm numb all over; the cold is getting to my brain. I'm starting to see things that aren't really there. Slowly I work my fingers into the snow and rock-hard mud and begin pulling myself up the hill, an inch at a time. I stop after a few seconds, totally exhausted. The bleeding has started again. I try to stop it.

I speak to my dogs, telling them to go for help. Ike jumps up and runs out of sight, his tail between his legs. Jake follows. They think I'm scolding them. I'm left alone. I keep asking God for a miracle, knowing it will take one now to save me.

I don't know how much time goes by. I lost my watch in the fall. I think I passed out for a spell. I think of my parents, both dead now, and wonder if soon I'll be joining them. In a way it would be a relief to be rid of this pain. "Lord, I hurt so badly. This old boy ain't going to make it."

Then, for a reason I can't explain, I feel a strength going through me, and I begin to move myself up the hill. It seems like someone actually has hold of my arm and is helping me. I'm still bleeding, though not so bad as before, and the pain has subsided a little. Somehow I make it back up to the large boulder and stop to catch my breath. Lying against the rock, I can feel a warm breeze coming from under the boulder.

* * *

Josh figures he's been on the hillside for about two hours, covering maybe 60 miles as he circles back and forth. It's 11:00 p.m. "Lord, I need Your help in locating my brother," he prays out loud. Then, over the noise of the snowmobile's engine, he thinks he hears a sound. He quickly turns off the motor and listens. There it is again, a shrill baying. "Dogs or coyotes," Josh decides, and reaches for the switch. Then there it is again, only louder this time. It seems to be coming his way.

In a few minutes Josh recognizes Ike and Jake, running straight for him. When they get within a few feet, they turn and run the other way. Josh follows the dogs up the valley to the cove. After a mile and a half, Josh begins to wonder if they're leading him on a wild goose chase.

Suddenly the dogs seem to vanish right into a huge boulder straddling the trail. Josh quickly cuts off the engine and gets off the snowmobile. He shines his flashlight around and calls my name. He thinks he hears a low moan coming from behind the rock. He nearly faints at what he sees. He thinks I'm dead, but then sees a slight fluttering of an eyelid.

"Don't move!" he says. "I'll have you out of these mountains in no time."

It's now 3:15 a.m. I've been on this hillside for nearly 24 hours. Somehow Josh loads me onto the snowmobile and heads out of that place. The storm has turned into a full-blown blizzard, piling snow up into large drifts.

Josh reaches for the emergency radio mike and calls the dispatcher. "Have an ambulance meet me at the junction of Highway 7 and Route 519!" That's eight rough miles away.

Topping the last hill, Josh sees flashing lights in the distance. He makes a turn onto the highway and stops in back of the ambulance. The emergency team takes over. As they slip me into the ambulance, my eyes open. "Thank you, brother, for saving my life. Next to God, I owe you everything."

Josh clasps my hand. "All you owe me is to get better."

"Take care of my dogs," I say, and pass out again.

The ambulance disappears, and the night is still and dark again. Josh looks skyward. "Thank You, Jesus."

INCREDIBLE
ADVENTURES

2

DANGEROUS DEWEY,

THE MOST WANTED MAN IN MARYLAND

by Jack Calkins

MY DAD SPENT most of his time in the Maryland State Penitentiary. He even got me in once or twice. Being the chief psychologist in a maximum security prison meant he got to analyze some pretty heavy dudes.

My childhood was filled with stories about prison riots, hunger strikes, padded cells—and executions. I don't recommend that kind of childhood for everybody, but the Lord taught me some incredible things through my dad.

One prisoner my father tried hard to help was a guy named Dewey.* He'd been convicted of armed robbery and attended one of my dad's psychotherapy groups.

Dewey learned to trust Doc, as the prisoners called my dad. He was one of the few people Dewey would ever trust in his life.

I was about 10 years old when Dewey escaped. Everyone was looking for him. The governor even called out the Army to help. Being considered armed and dangerous, Dewey became the most wanted man in the state of Maryland. FBI men and state and local police combed the streets of Baltimore looking for dangerous Dewey. But nobody could find him, and there was only one man Dewey would ever surrender to.

The black telephone in the dining room rang just after sundown. I remember it was getting dark and a storm had blown in. Mom answered, and motioned for Dad to come take the call.

What I remember of the conversation went something like this: "Where are you? Don't move. I should be there in about 25 minutes. OK." He walked over to the closet at the bottom of the stairs, pulled out a thin khaki raincoat, and while buttoning it up without raising his eyes, said, "If I'm not back in one hour, call the police." As he opened the door, the wind blew in a sheet of rain. Dad slammed the door tight behind him.

We lived in a row house in northeast Baltimore, in a neighborhood of mostly brick houses with cement porches and sidewalks. The lightning lit up the slate roofs as the thunder bounced endlessly from one side of the street to the other, the kind of stuff movie sets try to copy.

My mom majored in cool. She was used to craziness, but this was something else.

"What're you gonna do, Mom?" I asked.

"Wait," she smiled back.

But how long?

A half hour went by. The storm got real mean outside. Even the light from the street lamp couldn't dent the darkness. I pressed my face against our front window. The pane was cold, and I wondered if Dad was.

When the hour was almost over I whined, "When you gonna call, Mom?" She crocheted another row, pushed her glasses back up her nose, and sighed, "Not yet."

Another 15 minutes. "Now, Mom?"

"Let's just give him a few more minutes, honey."

My nerves were fried!

An hour and 25 minutes after Dad had pulled away into

the blackness, he returned. I moved to the front window and watched two glistening figures come toward the house. Dad had him.

He pushed Dewey in the front door like some stray cat that didn't know how to accept hospitality. Dewey plastered himself up against the wall behind the door. He looked . . . scared! My 10-year-old mind said, *Scared?* The most wanted man in the state was standing, shaking, dripping water on our living room floor.

"This is the nicest house I've ever been in, ma'am," he softly choked to my mother.

"Take Mr. Dewey upstairs and get him shaved and showered, Jack," Dad said as he tossed his hat on the bannister and stroked my head.

Sure, why not? I thought to myself as I got my first whiff of Dewey. *Boy, he must have hidden the past 14 nights in a trash can!*

He had.

Dewey was soaked to the skin. Old tobacco stench, booze, and garbage odor wafted through our little white-tiled bathroom. As I handed Mr. Dewey my dad's Gillette razor and shaving cream, it occurred to me how uncertain this whole situation was.

After a silent shower, we emerged from the steam-filled cavern. Mr. Dewey was transformed. His gaunt frame made a valiant effort to fill Dad's baggy pants. Then we went down the stairs and through the living room and made our entrance into the dining room. Mom had fixed some burgers and fries. Dewey smiled sheepishly and sat down as Mom scooted his chair toward the plate.

I distinctly remember the catsup dripping down the corner of Dewey's mouth onto the napkin he'd tucked into my dad's flannel shirt. That moment will remain with me forever. There he sat, peaceful, contented, under control, *and* the most wanted man in Maryland. Well, Maryland would have to wait, 'cause dessert was next.

Suddenly the front door smashed open as if the lock

hadn't existed! I'd never seen a real machine gun before. Especially one pointed in my general vicinity. It looked heavier than I'd imagined.

One of our neighbors had seen our car pull up, and recognized Dewey. They didn't know if we were in danger or not, so they called the cops. And here they were, dripping on the same spot Dewey had.

"Get your hands up!" the sergeant shouted at the criminal. Dewey wiped the vanilla ice cream off his lips as he pushed the chair back and stood up. His face looked petrified. Now he was dangerous. It was the first time I'd been afraid since Dad returned.

It was standard operating procedure for any suspect to be frisked immediately. Everything happened so fast, though, the police must have forgotten. But Dewey hadn't. He was handcuffed, and as the officers were escorting him through our lockless front door he quickly leaned over and pulled an eight-inch shiv (that's a homemade knife) from his boot. Holding it by the blade, he handed it to my father while sneering at the sergeant.

Mr. Dewey could have carved us up. But his faith in my father tamed him. The most wanted man in the state had held my hand, let me lead him around like a puppy, and even apologized to me for the way he smelled. Kindness is sure powerful stuff.

Later in life, God's loving-kindness tamed me. Memories of ol' Dewey helped me appreciate the faithfulness of my heavenly Father's love. Whenever I'm tempted to wallow in self-righteous religion, I remember that crazy night, and that it was my father's faithfulness that had made all the difference.

It still does.

---

*I've changed the name to protect the guilty.

ESCAPE ROUTE

by Bonnie Koncz

MARIA! Peter! Come to supper," Mother Miller called. As the two children raced into the kitchen they nearly collided in the doorway. Laughing, they sat down at the table.

"What's for dinner?" asked Peter, looking up at Mother as she took the pots off the stove.

"Cabbage and noodles."

"Oh, good!" exclaimed Maria. "Give me lots."

"Well, leave some for *me*," teased Peter. Mother sat down and asked the blessing, and soon every plate was filled from the steaming casserole.

"Children," said Mother, "I have something to tell you. It's very important, and I must ask you not to tell anyone."

"What is it? What is it?" they chorused.

"You know that our country has been taken over by another government. Food is difficult to get, and prices are making it hard for people to buy what they need, if the stores even have it."

"Yes," said Peter. "Uncle Carl's store was taken from him, and people who once owned their homes must now pay rent to live in them."

"That's happened to lots of people," said Maria. "I wish the enemy soldiers would go back home. It's scary to see them marching through the streets!"

"I'm afraid they won't be going," said Mother. "Many of our people have died trying to force them out. But they are here to stay now, and I'm afraid life will never be quite the same. Even though things have begun to settle down, I fear for what may come in the future, especially as you grow older. That is why I have made my decision—we must leave."

"You mean just leave our city?" asked Peter.

"No. I mean we must leave our country entirely. Many people have already escaped, and others will be trying. I've prayed a long time over this," said Mother.

"But Mother," cried Maria, "haven't the border guards killed people who have tried? Oh, Mother! I don't want to go!"

Mother put her arms around both her children and held them tight. "Don't be afraid. God will watch over us whether we stay here or whether we go elsewhere, and I believe it is in His plan for us to go. A man will come to the house tomorrow and explain what we are to do. Now as soon as we finish eating, I want you to get ready for bed."

Morning was slow in coming for two children who waited to learn what their future would be. As the sun started to filter through the windows, Peter and Maria got up and dressed. They could hear the sounds of breakfast downstairs.

"Good morning, children!" greeted Mother. "Our meal is ready." As they sat down to bowls of hot cereal and warm cinnamon toast, they heard a knock at the door.

"That might be the man," said Mother. "The one I told you was coming. Peter, answer the door. But don't say anything. Let him speak first. It's always possible that someone has discovered our plans. Even neighbors can't be trusted anymore. The government is rewarding those who turn in others as traitors."

Peter opened the door, and there stood a short man with graying hair. "Good morning," he said.

"Good morning, sir," said Mother, stepping up next to Peter. "It is rather early. Can we help you?"

"Are you—are you Mrs. Miller?"

"What is it you want?" asked Mother.

"My—my name—my name is George. I came to—Is there anyone else here?" He seemed to be nervous, as if he had doubts about the Miller family.

"No, we are the only ones. Have you come to help us?" After talking a few minutes they were convinced of each other's sincerity. The plan was laid out.

"I know the escape route by heart," he said. "A friend who has already crossed over showed me the way before he left. Three other people will be going with me, besides your family. We must walk to the border. Anyone in a vehicle would have to go on the main roads and would be more easily discovered. Don't bring any suitcases or sacks, and don't carry any household items with you. You must leave everything behind. Come only in the clothes you are wearing, and a coat. You won't be able to bring any food along either. We must avoid all appearances of being on some type of journey. By all means be casual. I will meet you at the edge of the forest near the water tower. On the other side of the forest is the border. We leave in three days."

As Mother closed the door behind the man, she looked weary. She had not anticipated leaving in only three days. The seriousness of it all weighed heavily on her.

"Mother? Are you all right?" asked Peter and Maria.

"Yes. I just want everything to go well. It will be hard, you know. It's a long way to the border, and we're not sure what we will find when we get there. We must remember every step of the way to be brave and have faith. Do you understand?"

Two nights later a frightened little family prayed and planned together.

"Children," whispered Mother the next morning as she gently shook each shoulder. "Get up. This is the day."

Quickly they dressed in their everyday clothes. Mother had fixed a large meal, not knowing how long it would be before they would eat again. She had the children wash the dishes, and while they were busy cleaning up, she looked around at the things she must leave behind, never to see again. The family pictures, the handmade linens, the little mementos passed down through the family for so many years. It was so hard to leave it all behind when each little possession had a special meaning. "Mother," said Maria as she and

Peter came out of the kitchen, "couldn't we each take just *one* favorite thing with us?"

"I'm afraid not. It all must stay, and we must go." With one last look they closed the door behind them.

Out into the street they filed for their long walk through town. "Try to be casual, try to be casual," rang in their minds with every step. Mother greeted the baker who was standing in the doorway of the local store.

"Good morning."

"Good morning. A nice day today."

"Yes, it is," answered Mother, hoping he would not expect her to stop and talk further.

"Hello there," called a neighbor as she was sweeping her porch. "Come see me later today. I'm baking a cake and want to give you some. I've been saving the ingredients for a long time."

"How nice of you," Mother called out. Each person was greeted and a word or two was exchanged as the three passed the familiar houses of their friends. *Why are so many people out and about already?* wondered Mother. After several blocks they no longer saw people they knew. But still Peter felt as if he had a big sign tacked on his shirt that said "Escaping." It was hard not to feel self-conscious.

Some soldiers walked past on their morning patrol, and Peter thought back over the events of the past months. Resistance to the invaders had been strong. Civilians fought alongside the military to push the enemy troops out. There seemed to be fighting all over the city, and at times the streets literally flowed with blood. Finally the enemy withdrew, and there were great cries of freedom and victory. The guns were put away, and everyone was celebrating. But they were taken by surprise when the enemy tanks came rolling back, this time to win.

Mother is right to want us to leave, thought Peter. *And God will surely help us.*

"How much longer till we are out of the city?" Maria asked.

"Very soon, I think," answered Mother. "A few more blocks, and we'll be outside the city limits."

Finally they came to the forest. How beautiful it was. The autumn leaves had covered the floor with a crinkly carpet, and the bare arms of the trees seemed to reach to the heavens. George, with two other men and a young woman, was waiting.

"Over here—hurry!" he said. The group gathered together for final instructions. "It is very easy to get lost in this forest, but I am sure of the way, so please do not get separated from me. I cannot come back for you." Mother pulled the children close to her. "We must go as quickly and as quietly as possible. That won't be easy with these dry leaves, but do your best. There may be soldiers in the forest or people working, and I'd like to avoid meeting them. We'd have a hard time explaining what we were doing here. Now follow me. Make sure the children keep up."

As quiet as the travelers tried to be, the leaves made a noisy *crunch crunch*. They stopped to hide a few times when rustling leaves told of the approach of a hunting party. Through the dense forest they wound their way—sometimes on the well-worn deer paths, sometimes straight through brush and foliage. It was hard and tiring hour after hour, but the little group was determined to keep going. Deep in the forest the incredible beauty made it hard at times for Peter to remember what a desperate situation they were in. Suddenly George stopped. "I've changed my mind," he said quietly. "I can't go on. Continue on if you want to, but I won't be going with you."

"But you can't do that!" exclaimed Mother, as everyone pressed around. "At least tell us the way."

"I can tell you nothing," he said. "I have decided to go back. If you are caught and they find out who was leading you, it will mean my finish. I just cannot tell you," he cried. The men began to argue with him, but he bolted down the path and back through the forest.

"Mr. George!" Peter yelled and started to run after him.

"No!" said one of the men. "We can't go after him. He's not going to tell us anything, and I'm not about to turn back."

"But what can we do?" questioned Mother. "We have no

idea which way to go!"

"We know the general direction of the border. And I think we are closer to the border than to the city. Maybe we have a chance."

"But we don't know where to cross over," said the young woman. "Without a guide we don't have a chance of coming out in the right spot. We're doomed before we try."

The older man agreed. But Mother, remembering her earnest prayer to God to guide her family, finally sided with the young man. Soon they were all in agreement to at least try, and off they started in the direction George had been leading them. With so many trees and such thick underbrush, it was hard to tell which way to go. For several days they walked through the forest, only to find themselves retracing their steps.

"We're going in circles," moaned the young woman. "We are hopelessly lost." Now more unsure than ever, they gathered together in a small clearing to talk. The wind blew and the leaves swirled around their feet.

"Mother," whispered Maria, and she tugged on her sleeve. Out into the clearing stepped two large men. They were dressed as woodsmen, and each had an ax slung over his shoulder. Mother knew that the men who worked in the forest were a rough bunch and would likely not have much sympathy with what they were trying to do. At the very least, they would be robbed of what little they had. At the worst . . .

"I didn't hear them coming, did you?" whispered the woman to Mother.

"You are looking for the border, aren't you?" asked one of the men as they walked over. No one said anything. "We know you are. *You*. Come with us." They took the older man from the group and disappeared with him into the bushes.

"Oh, no!" cried Mother. "I'm afraid they'll kill him for sure. Why did they take him?"

"Let's run," suggested the young woman. "We have to try to get away. Think of your children."

Unable to decide what to do, they stood and waited. They

didn't want to abandon the old man, who had suffered a great deal in their wanderings the past few days. In a short while the woodsmen returned, and behind them walked the old man with a happy smile on his face.

"I can't believe they didn't harm him," said Mother. "I wonder what they want?" The old man hurried over.

"They have told me everything!" he exclaimed. "We can get to the border for sure now. The way will be clear."

"But remember," cautioned one of the woodsmen, "don't try to cross over until exactly 4:00. That's when the guards go into their stations for one or two minutes to change posts and receive orders."

"How can we tell you how grateful we are?" said Mother as she turned to the man standing close to her. "I have a little money and a gold watch. Please take them as a small payment for helping us." She tried to press them into his hand.

The woodsman smiled and looked at his companion. "No, you keep them. We don't need money."

The little band of refugees hugged each other and turned to thank their unexpected helpers. They could not see them in any direction and heard no sounds on the pathway.

Following the directions they had been given, they reached the border a little before 4:00. The winter sun, now slowly disappearing, was casting its last rays of light on the wire fence that marked the border. Right in front of them was a hole in the fence. They took their coats off to make it easier to pass through. They knew that the fence, if touched, would automatically ring a bell in the guardhouse. From their position in the bushes, they saw the guards in their towers, machine guns on their backs. At exactly 4:00 the guards left their posts and went inside the building.

"Now!" said the old man. As quickly as they could, each one scurried through the hole. On the other side Mother grabbed Maria's and Peter's hands and started running. The field was icy cold and wet, and the children slipped repeatedly. "Keep going!" urged Mother. Soon she was half dragging them behind her.

It wasn't long before the guards reappeared. Shots rang out all around. Peter glanced down the field and saw other people scrambling to get across the border. On they went, running as fast as they could. Soon it was completely dark.

"Look!" cried Mother. On the far side of the field small lights began flashing, showing them which way to come. "We're almost there, children. Keep going."

Just when Peter and Maria thought they couldn't take another step, they reached the other side and were met by friendly faces. They were exhausted and cold, and their stomachs ached with hunger, but they were glad to be safe.

"God has surely guided us here," said Mother, and they bowed together in prayer.

DANGER AT MIDNIGHT

by Steffi Adams

IOWA. *JULY 6, 1881.* Fifteen-year-old Kate Shelley gathered the damp clothes into her apron and raced toward the cottage. "That was close," she said as a fat raindrop plopped smack-dab onto the top of her head and rolled down the center part in her long brown hair.

Kate scurried into the cottage just as the darkening skies spilled open. Slamming the door and bolting it against the wind, she ran to the window. There she joined her younger sisters, Mayme and Margaret, and her brother John to watch the sheets of slanting rain pour from black, boiling clouds.

The old clock ticked away the hours and still the rain fell. In the blinding flashes of lightning, Kate watched gentle Honey Creek transform itself into a swollen, rushing monster.

"Mother, you should see the valley. It's like a huge bowl filled with water," Kate said. She shivered. "You don't think the trains will be making their runs, do you?"

Mrs. Shelley pushed a strand of hair off her flushed forehead and glanced up from the sizzling pan on the cookstove to answer her daughter. Then, seeing jagged streaks of lightning through the window, she shut her eyes and stopped up her ears with her index fingers. "Oh, I hate thunder!" she said. "That next one's going to be close." Sure enough, a series of booming thunderclaps shook the cottage.

When the rumbling skies were calmer, Mrs. Shelley opened her right eye, then her left. "Thank God, we're still safe," she told the children. "We'll just hope and pray that no one is out in this storm."

The hours crept by as the Shelleys watched and prayed for the storm to end. The clock was striking 11:00 p.m. when Kate suddenly cocked her head toward Honey Creek Bridge.

"Mother, listen. Did you hear that bell?" Kate asked. "There it goes again. That couldn't be a train, could it? In this storm?"

As she spoke, they heard a thundering, earthshaking crash, followed by the terrible hissing of steam. Even the raging winds took notice and were shaken into a gravelike stillness.

"Oh, Mother! It's No. 11. They've gone down Honey Creek Bridge!" Kate shouted. "Someone must help them." She thought for a moment, then squared her shoulders. "I must help them."

Mrs. Shelley shook her head, and gathered the frightened younger children around her rocker. "I can't let you go out in this storm, child. I lost your brother by drowning, and I don't intend to lose you, too."

"But what if I can save someone's life? Shouldn't I even try?" Kate asked. She picked up a small miner's lamp and hung it in the frame of an old lantern.

Mrs. Shelley grabbed Kate's arm. "Child, you can't even swim. Why, you're deathly afraid of water. How do you expect to help anyone?"

"What am I to do, Mother? If Pa and James were alive, they'd go. But they aren't here. Don't you see? I have to go." Kate began filling the lamp with kerosene. Seeing the worry lines engraved on her mother's face, she said, "Haven't you always taught us that God makes strong the weakest . . . ?"

". . . and He makes the poorest of us able to endure much for His merciful purposes," Mrs. Shelley said, finishing her favorite saying. The worry lines were completely erased and her face grew peaceful. "Yes, I believe that, Kate."

She handed Kate an old straw hat and added, "Go then— in the name of God—and do what you can. We'll pray God to keep you from harm."

Kate kissed her mother and unbolted the door. "Now don't fret. I'll be just fine," she said. Bracing herself against the fierce, screaming winds, she lifted her skirt and splashed out into the rising waters.

When her eyes had adjusted to the inky blackness, Kate scrambled up the steep bank behind the cottage. Nearby, she saw a section of track that had not been flooded by the rushing, muddy water. Swinging her lantern before her, Kate stumbled blindly down the tracks toward the collapsed bridge.

Minutes later, Kate stood beside the swaying sections of Honey Creek Bridge. "Is anyone down there?" she shouted into the howling wind.

A burst of lightning lit up the steaming twisted wreckage, and Kate spied two men in the flood waters 25 feet below. Both men were hanging onto the overhanging branches of stout trees.

Frantically, Kate swung her lantern from left to right. "Yoo-hoo!" she yelled. "Here I am! Up here!"

One of the men saw Kate's lantern and called out to her again and again. Each time his words were muffled by the whistling wind and the crack of thunder.

Hoping that he would understand her, Kate yelled, "I'm going to Moingona for help. Hang on. I'll be back."

Slipping in the cool, oozing mud, Kate muttered, "What have I gotten myself into?" She trembled at the thought of the one-and-one-fourth mile trip to the station house, and of the swollen Des Moines River that lay between her and the town.

At that instant, a terrible thought flashed through Kate's weary mind. The pusher that had crashed had been checking the tracks between Moingona and Boone. *That means the midnight express will be coming into Moingona soon,* she thought. *I've got to warn Agent McIntyre about the danger.*

Holding the lantern above her head, Kate ran down the path beside Honey Creek. With every passing second her heart pounded harder until she thought it would surely burst. "What time is it?" she wondered aloud. "Oh, dear God, let me make it in time."

Precious minutes flew by as Kate followed the lantern's faint, flickering beam. *What if the train should catch me on the bridge? No, I won't think of that.*

In a sudden flash of lightning, Kate saw the 500-foot Des Moines River Bridge just ahead. Overflowing with foul-smelling rubbish and broken fence posts, the river slapped at the bridge's unprotected railroad ties. At every movement the swaying timbers groaned as if in pain.

Kate stiffened her back and took a deep breath. She put one foot on the slippery bridge and, holding out her arms, balanced herself like a tightrope walker. "Now don't look down, Kate," she whispered.

As she stepped onto the bridge, a gust of wind playfully fingered the lantern's tiny flame, then snuffed it out. Kate sucked in her breath and froze in the sudden darkness.

"God makes strong the weakest."

Instantly, her mother's saying captured Kate's runaway thoughts. She felt the prayers of her family covering her like one of Mother's homemade quilts. Trusting in God, Kate knelt and began crawling along over the rough, wooden railroad ties.

Time after time Kate's bulky, sopping-wet skirt caught on bent nails and she had to brace herself to keep from falling into the raging waters below. Sharp splinters jabbed into her bloody knees. Still she ignored the beating winds and crawled inch by painful inch across the bridge, every breath a prayer for her safety and for the lives of those on the train.

Kate was almost halfway across the bridge when a burst of lightning lit up the angry flood waters around her. There, in the swirling waters, Kate saw a monstrous uprooted tree hurtling toward the bridge.

She gripped the rail so tightly that her knuckles turned deathly white. "Oh, God," she prayed. "Help me." She shut her eyes, waiting for the terrible collision sure to come.

Foam and icy water sprayed over her as the tree's branches scraped the bridge. The bridge itself pitched from side to side like a bucking bronco while Kate held on with all her might. As she prayed, the bridge heaved and the tree shot forward under it, leaving the wobbly bridge unharmed.

Kate's legs felt as useless as wet noodles. Still, she inched her way toward solid ground. She could have cried with relief when she finally crawled off the bridge, but picking herself up, she sprinted the fourth of a mile to the station house.

"Stop the express! Honey Creek Bridge is out," Kate shouted when she finally burst into the station house.

The men just stared at the wild-eyed, dripping figure. "The girl's touched in the head," night operator Ike Fansler said, shaking his head.

Agent McIntyre disagreed. "It's Mike Shelley's oldest daughter," he said. "The girl ought to know."

Quickly Ike sat down at the telegraph keys while another worker rushed to light the red warning lantern beside the tracks. Nearby, a waiting engineer blew the whistle of his own sidetracked pusher engine. As the shrill whistle pierced the night, sleepy townsmen poured from their houses carrying ropes and shovels.

"Kate, do you feel up to going back with us?" Agent McIntyre asked.

"I'll try, sir," Kate said. Her head was throbbing and she really wanted to lie down between crisp, sun-dried sheets. But for now she had a job to finish. And with God's help, finish it she would.

Kate did finish the job. Before the night was over, she watched the townsmen rescue both the engineer and the brakeman of the wrecked pusher engine. Not until days later, when the searchers had discovered the bodies of the last two crewmen, did Kate collapse.

For many days Kate hovered near death. She knew nothing of the poems and the newspaper articles being written about her. When she awoke and her mother told her about the excitement, Kate just said, "Imagine that. Me, a heroine!"

Yes, Kate Shelley was a national heroine, and people could not thank her enough. From the grateful express passengers came several hundred dollars. The railroad company and its employees rewarded Kate with a gold watch and a lifetime pass to ride the trains.

Even people whom Kate had never met helped the Shelleys. In 1882 the Iowa General Assembly voted to give Kate a gold medal and $200. The Chicago *Tribune* collected money to pay off the family's debts while Frances Willard, the temperance leader, raised enough funds to send Kate to Simpson College.

Kate didn't expect all the fuss to last, but in 1903, 22 years later, people still remembered her. When she became station master at Moingona, a train always stopped at the cottage to take her to and from work. And at her death in 1912, the railroad company sent a special train to carry her family and friends to the funeral.

Today a sturdy bridge, the Kate Shelley Bridge, spans the Des Moines River at a spot four miles from the site of Kate's crossing. On the bridge is a plaque which reads: "Hers is a deed bound for legend . . . a story to be told until the last order fades and the last rail rusts."

Kate Shelley is still remembered.

MINISTER TO BANDITS

by Barbara Westphal

HALT! GET OFF your horse! Hand me the reins!"

It was a holdup.

Angel, the teenage evangelist, had traveled alone on horseback for three and one-half days searching for a group of Sabbathkeepers deep in the mountains of Mexico.

"I organized a Sabbath school with 20 members," an active lay member had told him. "You will have to travel several days to get there, but you must go and visit them. The place is a hideout for criminals. Everyone there has killed somebody. That's why they live where the law can't find them."

Angel couldn't find them either. Somewhere he must have taken a wrong turn. He was lost, and now the armed bandit was making him dismount and demanding, "What's in your saddlebag?"

"A projector with reels and a battery adapter."

The bandit rummaged around in the leather bag and eyed the strange contraption. "Looks like a small cannon to me. What's it for?"

"It's to show pictures so that—"

"Come with me and we'll see. If you're fooling me, I'll break your neck."

There was nothing to do but follow the bandit to his hideout. Angel mounted his horse again, but the bandit kept the reins and led him along a well-hidden path through the trees and rocks. For two hours they struggled down a steep canyon. When they reached the bottom, the bandit whistled. One by one from behind trees, rough men appeared.

"What did you bring that fellow here for?" the leader complained.

"He says he has a picture outfit with him. If he doesn't, we'll kill him."

Both Angel and his horse were hungry, for they hadn't eaten all day, but the captain said, "It's dark enough to begin. We need some amusement, so let's get going."

As he set up the simple equipment, Angel remembered he had only two lightbulbs with him. He prayed that those bulbs, which often became overheated and broke, would last. He knew his life depended on pleasing the robber band.

What reel should he choose? Again he prayed, and then he selected "The Plan of Salvation." He spoke straight from his heart about each picture. The script could be read in 35 minutes, but he talked on and on. He began to hear subdued exclamations from the hardened men.

"O God, have pity on me!"

"Forgive me!"

"What a miserable life I've lived!"

When he finally stopped it was midnight. At last the captain said, "Are you hungry?"

They prepared a meal of beans and enchiladas, and after another hour they told him he could rest. But where?

"You sleep by me," ordered the gang leader. The bandit chief lay down on a bed and slipped his big machete and his .45 pistol under the blanket he used for a pillow. Under the bed was his Mauser (a rifle).

Angel knelt down and prayed before he lay down on the bed beside the thief. About 6:30 a.m. he woke up and found his horse, hoping to make a fast getaway. He was saddling when the others began to awaken.

"You mustn't go! You can't go!" they shouted. "You are our prisoner until you finish telling us about all the pictures you have."

They unsaddled his horse and led it away.

After a breakfast of hot tortillas the men sat down and Angel studied all morning with them. He showed another reel in the afternoon, and that evening between 8:00 and 1:00 he presented two more.

Next morning he attempted to ride away again, but it was no use. They kept him with them for three days and four nights.

"Now you can go if you promise not to tell the authorities about us."

They sent one of their men as a guide. As they rode along together for seven hours, Angel talked to the bandit about changing his life and becoming a Christian. How happy he felt when the man said, "Be sure the seed you have sown will bear fruit in my life at least, if not in the lives of the others. I am going to leave the gang and start a new life."

He lovingly touched the Bible that Angel gave him, then set him on the road toward the village that he had been looking for before his capture. At the parting of the ways the bandit asked, "When will you return?"

"I'll come through Huahatla in three or four months," the evangelist promised. They knelt down and prayed together, then put their arms around each other in a tearful embrace.

"I'll change my life and will meet you again" were the last words of his guide.

Angel found the little Sabbath school group for which he had been searching and stayed a few days to give them special instruction.

Exactly four months later he returned to Huahatla, wondering if he would find his bandit friend again.

He was there, but how different! Angel scarcely recognized him. Not only were his clothes different—neat and clean—but his face was happy and honest instead of dark and fierce. He had studied the Bible and the lessons Angel had given him, and he was ready to be baptized. He had gone back to his wife and children and was eager to tell the gospel story to others.

Angel is now a pastor in Mexico City. He says, "What a providence it was that I lost my way and was a prisoner of bandits!"

THE NIGHT THE STARS FELL

by Josephine Edwards

WHEN MY GRANDMOTHER was just 10 years old, her father wanted to go out West. His farm was in the hills of North Carolina, and the land was so hilly it was discouraging to try to get a good crop. People told him of the broad, flat, fertile lands in a place called Indiana, where the soil was rich and productive. So the family sold out and got ready to go.

Challons—that's my grandma's dad—had written ahead and purchased a homestead of 160 acres bordering a creek, the water of which never failed.

With high hopes, the family packed up their beloved possessions in two huge covered wagons. No one dreamed of taking such journeys in a hurry in those days, for the road was bad and some of it had to be made as one went along.

They always stopped and camped at nightfall, as near to a stream as they could. While everyone did their appointed tasks, Janie, Grandma's mother, prepared food that tasted like ambrosia after a bone-jarring day in the lurching covered wagons.

When the memorable night of November 13, 1833, rolled around, the travelers were high in the Cumberlands, camped by the side of a swift, clear mountain stream. They had decided to camp here for a few days and wash clothes and gather in some food. There was a small town nearby, and the woods were near enough for Challons and his son Valen to get some deer and perhaps a pheasant and a wild turkey or two. Janie wanted to bake some bread ahead, too.

Pa and Ma and little Amby and Baby Ann slept in the first wagon. Margaret, my grandmother, slept alone in the second, while big brother Valen, rolled in a blanket, slept underneath the wagon, right on the ground.

They all went to bed early that night of November 13, 1833. Margaret and her mother had done a big washing in the stream, with the good homemade soap Janie had brought with her from the old home. Even as they went to bed, Margaret could see the clothes draped over the bushes, white patches in the darkness under the trees. Pa and Valen had been busy too. They had killed a deer, skinned it, and cut a lot of the meat in strips to dry, so it would last them for a long time. Smoked, dried deer meat was called jerked venison. Everyone was tired, so the beds, such as they were, felt very good on that night so long ago.

Margaret stretched out her young legs wearily between her mother's homespun sheets and drew the handwoven coverlid over her. She had gone to sleep with the twilight barely gone and the western sky still flushed with the red of sunset. She was awakened by Pa shaking her gently, yet urgently. She could hardly see his silhouette, it was so dark.

"Margaret, Margaret," he called softly, almost in the tone he would use if someone were dead. The girl sat up, her heart plunging in alarm. Was it Indians? Snakes? Bears? Wildcats? Mountain lions?

"What is it, Pa?" she cried. Then she noticed leaping lights dancing crazily over the wagon canvas. "Is the forest afire? Will we be burned?"

"I hope not, Peggy," her father said gently, using her baby

pet name. "I hope not. But it might be the last night we will ever see in this world."

By this time his face was lit up by the queer glow. Without asking any more questions, Margaret slipped out of the high wagon in her clean white night "shift," washed and dried in the sun only that day. She remembered years later that the grass was very wet, and the frogs were shrilling loudly down in the little pond near the stream.

She slipped her small cold hand into her father's big warm one, and together they went to the open place in the woods where the rest were gazing upward. Even Baby Ann was awake in Mother's arms, rubbing her small button of a nose sleepily. She was not alarmed in the least. Hadn't these two big people taken her through every fear she had ever known? But Amby, who was 7, had his face hid in Mother's white nightgown and was sobbing.

Margaret looked up as soon as she came out from under the thick laced branches of the trees. A cold hand of fear clutched at her heart.

The whole sky was ablaze with darting lights. It was as if the whole firmament was on the move. Every star seemed to be leaping, leaving a fiery trail right toward the place in the Cumberlands where she was standing. The sky was a vast riddle of blazing streaks, like a million flashes of lightning ripping through the sky at the same time.

Margaret began to tremble, not only from fear, but from the cold. Fog was as thick as cotton balls down in the valley, and the chill penetrated even to the highlands, but no one thought of creeping back into the warm feather beds in the wagons, though little Ann did go to sleep, and Janie put her into bed in the forward wagon.

Margaret never forgot that night, even though she lived well into the next century, and died almost 71 years after the night she saw the stars fall.

After a while, when the children began to get a little used to the awful sight, Amby started to walk around and look up a little. He had kept his head under his mother's shawl, sobbing with fear for a long time. Then Father started to talk to them.

"Children," he said, "do you remember that little pamphlet that someone brought to our house back there before we left North Carolina?"

"Yes, Pa," Valentine answered slowly. "You read it out loud. It was by a man who believed the Bible says that the Lord will come the second time in our day."

"Yes. As I remember, his name was William Miller," Challons answered slowly.

"I remember we didn't put too much faith in it at the time," Janie said defensively.

"No, we didn't, Janie, that's true," her husband answered. "You know, I have always avoided fanaticism; but this falling of the stars is something else again. I know it is set down some place in the Bible. I remember either reading it, or hearing it read. If the world is still standing in the morning, I will look it up."

Nothing more spectacular happened. Amby got tired, and crept off to bed. Finally Margaret went to the wagon just to lie down. But in spite of her resolutions, she dropped off to sleep. When she awoke late the next morning, breakfast was over and everyone was almost ready to move on. The oxen had been yoked, and Janie had packed everything.

"Oh, Ma," cried Margaret. "Why didn't you call me?"

"You looked too tired, my little one," answered Janie, understandingly. "But I saved you some porridge, and kept it hot in the embers."

With that Janie brought the girl a thick homespun cloth, wet in the stream to wash her face and hands. Then the bowl of porridge, feathery gray from fluffy wood ashes, was hastily wiped off and put into Margaret's hands. It was made of home-ground meal, and sweetened with wild honey from the bee tree Valen had discovered the week before. Clotted cream from old Clover, the yellow Jersey cow, was heaped on top. Before Margaret had finished her breakfast, the wagons were on their way westward, swaying and bumping and jogging.

Everywhere they passed, there were stories of the terrors

of the night before. The Negroes in a nearby plantation had had a prayer meeting that lasted all night. They weren't worth a cent in the cotton fields the next day, so people said. But the White folks didn't have too much to say, for they had been excited too at the queer thing that had happened to the world! A woman in one village had gone quite crazy, and had wandered all night in her nightgown. She had been found the next morning distraught and babbling.

Margaret listened to everything that was said, and to her father telling people in the trading post about William Miller, and of how he had heard he was preaching about the soon coming of the Lord up in York State.

At noontime, because they were stopped near the village, Janie cooked up a stew. One of the men in the village had brought in a deer, and one of the women brought a big piece to Janie with some corn bread and some Indian pudding. When they gathered around to eat, they were all talking about the falling of the stars, and what this one and that one in the village had said.

"That reminds me of tales I've heard my Grandma Marais tell about what happened when my own mother was just a babe in the cradle," Janie said. She had lifted the lid of the Dutch oven and was cutting the steaming corn bread for everyone to sop in their venison stew. A bowl of churn-fresh butter was set on some burdock leaves, and everybody spread it richly on every slice of bread, till it melted and ran down into their bowls of stew.

"What happened when your mother was a baby?" asked Margaret curiously, accepting her own hot wedge of buttered bread from her mother's busy hands.

Janie straightened her back and looked off toward the distant hills a long time before she answered.

"Grandma said that Grandpa had been off in the Army for a long time. Then he got a wound in his leg from the battle of King's Mountain. Uncle Jim helped him get his plantin' done for he never did get real pert again. The wound in his leg never healed up right till he was old. It gave him trouble till he died, especially in damp, cold weather.

"Grandma said it was in May. The crops were in and they were plowing like mad. The weeds had gotten ahead of them, but that morning, Grandma said she put her breakfast on early. Buckwheat cakes, she said she baked, and fried eggs, and sorghum molasses. I've got her long-legged griddle yet, and you've all eaten many a buckwheat cake baked on Grandma Marais' griddle. They had just got set down when Grandpa said 'Go to the door, Lessie, and see if a storm is brewing. It's gettin' pretty dark, like the sun's cloudin' over.'

"Grandma said she went to the door and looked out. It looked for all the world like it was coming night instead of being early in the morning."

"Aw, yes, I remember," her husband contributed then. "That was the famous Dark Day. My father was a drummer boy in the Army when it happened. He said that some of the soldiers almost went crazy with fear. They thought it was the day of judgment for sure."

"That is what my grandma told me," Janie answered. "She said the slaves hung around the houses weeping and mourning like children all day. And the White folks weren't much behind them in being afraid."

"Was it dark all day, Ma?" Valen asked curiously.

"Yes, sir, it was," Janie answered. "Grandma told me she lit candles, and no one went to the fields. The cows went to the shed, and the chickens flew up in the orchard trees and went to roost. She said that night was so dark you couldn't see your hand in front of your face, and the moon looked like a big pumpkin, glowing like phosphorus in the dark."

"That's written up in the Bible, too, same as the falling of the stars," Challons told them. Then he got up and got his ponderous Bible off the wagon seat where he had been reading. He began to read to them as they sat on the green grass around the cookpot, on that day more than 110 years ago. He had looked it all up as soon as it got daybreak on that morning. It had not been hard, for Challons had read the Bible through several times.

"Immediately after the tribulation of those days shall the sun be darkened, and the moon shall not give her light, and the stars shall fall from heaven, and the powers of the heavens shall be shaken" (Matt. 24:29).

Challons looked up from the big brass-bound leather book solemnly.

"Three of these signs have come to pass in our day," he said. "William Miller must have some truth at least, and I for one am going to look into it."

"What does it mean about the 'powers of heaven,' Pa?" asked Valen curiously.

"That I do not know, my son," answered Challons. "It has not taken place yet. But I believe it will happen, and we will know it if it does in our day. We must serve God, and be ready."

Challons, Janie, Margaret, yes, even Valentine and Amby, and Baby Ann all are dead. Their graves are sunken, and the stones are standing crooked and mossy, as if Satan would say, "See? All things continue as they did since the fathers fell asleep." But don't let him fool you!

Margaret got married after she reached Indiana, and her tenth child was Elizabeth, my own dear mother. Sixty-nine years after the falling of the stars, my mother heard and accepted the third angel's message. She, too, is sleeping, awaiting the trump of God and the awakening call of the Lord. She knew very well that the Lord will come at the appointed time. And so did my grandparents, and my greats, and great-greats, and great-great-greats, clear back to the Dark Day, May 19, 1780.

A TIME TO HEAL

by Melanie Scherencel

THE MORNING DAWNED cold. The sun broke across the pale-blue sky, the frost lightly fingering the lacy tops of the still-bare trees in our yard.

Grandpa had gone out to check the store to make sure everything was in place. He did that every morning while Grandma made breakfast. He didn't have far to walk; it was only a few hundred yards away.

Shivering, I bounced up and down as I watched Grandma put the biscuits in the oven.

"Cut that out, child," Grandma fussed. "It sounds like an earthquake in here." She laughed. "You're such a tomboy, Daisy. Just like your mother."

Smiling, I walked into the living room and leaned my head up against the big, cold window, waiting for Grandpa to come back to the house.

Before long, I saw Grandpa walking slowly home with his head down. He wasn't whistling like he usually did. When he arrived at the door, I opened it for him and said good morning. When he brushed past me like I wasn't there and headed for the kitchen, I knew something was terribly wrong. He was making a funny kind of snuffling noise. He was crying. I'd never seen him cry before, and it scared me.

"Whatever is the matter, William?" Grandma asked anxiously.

"They did it, Catherine," he said in a choked-up voice as he sat down. "The bootleggers. They were there last night— took the sugar and stuff they needed for the moonshine whiskey and left. We've been robbed, Catherine. The place is a mess."

He buried his head in his arms on the table and continued to sob out his frustration and sadness. I saw Grandpa wither before my eyes. He suddenly looked very old.

Grandpa would've done anything for anybody, and why anyone would do something like that to him filled me with a ragged kind of rage!

"I hate 'em," I said to myself. *"Whoever they are, I hate 'em."*

That afternoon Josiah Sparks came by the house.

"Hallo there, cutie," he said when he saw me. "I hear that y'all had some trouble around here last night."

"Bootleggers!" I spat the word out with venom. "Grandpa guesses they're from Cades Cove. They ransacked the store. Took what they wanted and left everything else a mess."

When Grandpa appeared around the side of the house, Josiah grinned widely, revealing the place where a front tooth should've been.

"Howdy, Lawson!" Josiah said. "Yer granddaughter here 'n' me was havin' a right nice little chat, wasn't we, cutie?" His grin became wider, and he winked at me. "Now tell me 'bout this bootlegger business, Lawson."

Josiah Sparks listened with interest as Grandpa related the story. He stroked his chin thoughtfully, then said with a frown, "Now ain't that too bad."

"Guess I'll go into Knoxville next Monday and replenish everything." Grandpa shook his head sadly. "I just don't know how I can do it, Josiah. I don't know how I can go on."

Several other neighbors stopped by to give their condolences. Grandpa thanked them all graciously for their concern, but the old sparkle was gone.

That evening all of us sat around the fire, including Uncle Earl, who was visiting.

"Daisy, did I ever tell you the story of the two girls who got lost in the woods and couldn't find their way out?" Uncle Earl asked me.

"No, I don't think so," I answered eagerly. "Tell me." Uncle Earl could tell some good stories.

"Well," Uncle Earl continued slowly with a twinkle in his eye, "they walked for days, and only got themselves lost. Well, they eventually ended up in the very center of the woods, where the ghosts live . . ."

"Earl Lawson!" Grandma scolded, horrified. "How dare you tell this child things like that before bedtime?"

"But Grandma," I protested.

Uncle Earl winked at me, and disappointed, I climbed the stairs to my bedroom.

Late that same night, after everyone had gone to sleep, I heard a sound. My heart began to pound rhythmically, and my toes tingled.

Grandma was right, I thought. *I'm hearing things.* I pulled the covers tight around my face and snuggled down into their warmth.

But suddenly I heard it again. Carefully and silently I pushed the covers back and slid out of bed. Tiptoeing across the room, I reached for my coat and boots. Not bothering to change, I pulled the heavy coat on over my pajamas and put the boots on my sockless feet.

The stairs creaked and groaned as I made my way down. Strangely, I had never noticed how noisy they were until now. *I've never tried to be this quiet coming down them before, either*, I mused to myself.

The sound seemed to be coming from outside. Unfortunately, the front door wasn't much more quiet than the stairs. As I eased out onto the porch, I could hear Uncle Earl's heavy breathing from where he slept on the couch.

All of a sudden I realized where the noise was coming

from. The store! I crept through the shadows along the edge of the woods until I was directly beneath the store's front window. My heart pounded with such force that I was sure they could hear it clear back at the house.

Whoever was inside, I could hear them talking. I stopped to listen.

"What's takin' y'all so long, Buck? Hurry up, wouldja?"

I was so astounded at the sound of the voice, I almost fell over. The voice belonged to none other than Josiah Sparks!

So it was him, I said to myself angrily. *That two-faced hypocrite!*

Suddenly I knew what I had to do. I had to get Grandpa and Uncle Earl. Silently I made my way back through the shadows toward the house. Just as I reached the porch, a twig snapped behind me, and a cold hand clamped around my mouth!

"What in the name of thunder are you doing outside this time of night?" a voice asked. Relieved, I whirled about and looked into the shadowed face of Uncle Earl.

"Oh, Uncle Earl!" I panted in a whisper. "I saw them! They're there! Josiah and his boys are the ones, Uncle Earl!"

"What are you talking about?" Uncle Earl asked quizzically. "Calm down and tell me."

"Bootleggers!" I said impatiently. "You've got to hurry! They're in the store!"

Without another word Uncle Earl turned and ran into the house. Moments later Grandpa came out, saddled up one of the horses, and rode for the sheriff. Uncle Earl had grabbed his gun and was headed for the store.

I snuck back to my place under the window to see what was going to happen.

"Now, Billy," Josiah said in a whiny voice, "don't you be tearin' everything out."

I cautiously raised my head to peek through the window.

"You know Lawson's gettin' old," Josiah continued. "Don't make things too hard on him."

Just then the door burst open.

"That's mighty kind of you, Josiah." Uncle Earl's voice was

as cold and hard as steel.

Josiah and his boys whipped around quickly, just in time to stare down the barrel of Uncle Earl's shotgun.

"Take it easy, boys," Uncle Earl said, frowning. "The sheriff should be here any minute now."

His hands in the air, Josiah swallowed, but said nothing. Billy's face crumpled, and he started to bawl. Buck stared uneasily at the shotgun in Uncle Earl's steady hands.

I almost felt sorry for them, but the picture of Grandpa's frail form slumped across the table kept flashing in my mind, and his sad voice. "They did it, Catherine . . ." No way. I could never feel pity for the people who made my grandpa cry. Hatred burned like a fire inside me once again.

It wasn't long before the sheriff arrived. After he had arrested Josiah and his boys and left again, Grandpa surveyed the mess in silence. "I reckon I'd better get started here," he said.

"I'll help you, Grandpa," I offered. He gave me a tired smile.

It took all of us till daybreak to get the store back in order. Exhausted after the long night, I fell asleep quickly, and didn't wake up until late afternoon.

The next day Uncle Earl came in with a discouraged look on his face.

"What's the trouble, Earl?" Grandpa asked.

"Sparks is a free man again, Pa," Uncle Earl said. "Seems the sheriff is a distant relative of his, and didn't like the idea of having kinfolk in jail. Josiah bribed him with a little moonshine whiskey and that's all it took. He's a free man."

I couldn't believe what I was hearing. It was so unfair!

Grandpa got up and walked out the door toward the barn. Had to do some thinking, I guess.

After he had gone, I flew into a passionate rage. "What about us? What about Grandpa's store? It's just not fair!"

Uncle Earl looked at me for a long time. "You're right," he said, "it's not."

The next day Grandpa was sick in bed. Deep down inside I knew it was Josiah Sparks' fault. I hated him. With everything I had inside me, I hated him.

Grandpa knew something was bothering me. Calling me into his room, he asked, "Daisy, is there something you'd like to talk about? It's as plain as day there's something wrong."

I burst into tears. "It's not fair, Grandpa!" I cried. "You've always done everything you could for other people. You've always been honest. But you got your store robbed. You're the one who's sick. Josiah is the bootlegger and thief. But he got out of jail! And he's still healthy."

"I know how you feel, Daisy," Grandpa said gently. "I had those same feelings. It took me a lot of thinking and prayer 'fore I could understand them myself." He paused. "In the Good Book it says that God lets the rain fall on the good and the bad, not just the good. But in another spot it says that everybody's going to get his own reward when the Lord comes. I reckon the best thing I can do is trust the Lord and let Him take care of it."

"I guess you're right, Grandpa," I said softly. I leaned over and kissed his weathered cheek. "Thanks."

Grandpa smiled as he watched me leave the room. He never recovered from the robbery, physically or financially.

Sometime later, as I sat by his grave, I knew that I still felt bitterness toward Josiah and his boys. I thought about what Grandpa had said, and started to cry. I ached so much inside that I wished my heart could break open and let the hurt pour out. But I knew he was right. All I could do was let the Lord take care of it.

I watched the sun slowly sink from the sky, leaving behind orange- and magenta-colored fragments of light that seemed to melt onto the horizon.

And the hate inside me began to dissolve.

LIFECHANGING DISCOVERIES

3

ONE MONTH, 4 DAYS TO LIVE

by Elva Gardner

CHANG YOUNG STOOD at a respectful distance back of his English master's chair in the dining room in India. Clad in a starched spotless white butler's uniform, he stood like a soldier at attention.

Chang Young was the perfect servant. He knew when to refill the master's cup of tea, when to pass the vegetables, when to bring the evening paper, when to talk and when to keep still. There were many other things he knew, such as which shirt the master would like laid out, just when the slippers were wanted, the temperature of the bath water, and which guests were welcome and how to get rid of those not wanted.

He also knew how to gather news around the tea plantation and how to keep the family secrets.

Chang Young was from China, and had held his present job as butler and valet to the master on the Indian tea plantation several years.

Now he stood behind his master's chair in the dining

room waiting for just the right moment to speak. He had just refilled the cup of tea.

"Master." (He spoke in low tones.) "One month I go China. I train new servant for master before I go."

The master did not turn to look at Chang Young. This was their usual way of talking with Chang Young standing behind him.

"Are you looking for a wife, Chang Young? I suppose you *are* lonely. But there is no need for you to go to China to get a wife. I will pay the fare of a Chinese girl to come here."

"I no get married, master. I go China stay. I teach new servant to take good care of master."

"What's the matter? Aren't you getting wages enough? I'll raise your pay. How much am I paying you now?"

"Master pay plenty now. I no want more money. I go China stay."

Now the master lost his patience.

"Chang Young, you aren't going to China to stay. Do you understand? If you want more pay or more help, just say so. I don't want to hear any more of this nonsense."

Chang Young was quiet, and the master was sorry he had become angry.

"Chang Young, I was angry. Forgive me."

Chang Young was still silent.

"Chang Young, why do you want to go to China?"

"I no can say. Master will laugh at me."

"Chang Young, I promise not to laugh at you. Tell me why you must go."

"Master, I go China. I die."

The master stopped eating.

"Are you ill? Why haven't you told me? You shall have the best doctors."

"I no sick, master."

"Then what is this nonsense about dying?"

"Master, one month, 4 days today, I die."

"How do you know you are going to die one month and 4 days from today?"

"Master, in my country I have brother. He have wife and children. I have no family. My brother now in prison. He sentenced to die one month, 4 days. In my country brother can die for brother. I go China, die for brother."

* * *

Now another servant stands back of the master's chair, fills his cup of tea, lays out the shirts, and keeps his secrets.

Greater love hath no man than he lay down his life.

A long time ago a Son said to His Father. "I go; I die for my brother." Was that brother you?

THE TATTOO

by Mary Louise Kitsen

IT WAS REALLY hard to imagine a lady with a tattoo! But Ruth had one, and to my youthful eyes, it was an amazing thing indeed.

Ruth was an elderly woman. Her son was a businessman in Hartford, the capital city of my home state of Connecticut. He had arranged to bring his mother to the United States from Europe. She had not fitted into his lifestyle, however, so he did what he considered his duty in a roundabout way. He purchased a small home for her in my small hometown.

In the beginning I didn't pay very much attention to Ruth. What was there to notice? She fussed about her house and yard contentedly but did not go out of her way to make friends. Not that she was unpleasant. She'd smile and speak in a quiet manner when spoken to. However, she made no effort to be close to anyone.

Then one day I came home from school, riding my bike and thinking happy thoughts, and Ruth entered my life. It was one of those days when you feel good about everything. I had much to be glad about. World War II was newly over and my favorite cousin would soon be home from overseas duty. I was convinced that the world would now live in peace forever.

I turned into my yard, and Mama looked up from her garden. "Honey, Ruth wants to know if you'll run some errands for her each week. She'd pay you two dollars."

Two dollars! It seemed like a lot of money to me. I was already mentally spending it. "Sure," I said. "When do I start?"

"As soon as you freshen up," Mama told me. "Then you can go talk to Ruth."

Ruth motioned me into her kitchen. It didn't look anything like our kitchen at home. Our kitchen was always in a state of disorder. Ruth's kitchen was so neat it was almost as though no one lived there. "Do you promise to be a girl I can rely on?" the elderly lady asked me.

I nodded.

"I hope so. I don't have money to waste, though I will pay you fairly as long as you do your best. I need a few things from the store. Here's the list and money."

The list had but a few items. I made a quick trip to the neighborhood grocery, picked up the things, paid for them, and put the bag in the basket of my bike. When I carried the bag into the kitchen, Ruth began immediately to put the groceries away. That's when I noticed the tattoo.

It was on her arm, just above her hand. I wondered what kind of lady would have a tattoo. The only tattoos I'd seen before were on Mike, the man my dad hired when he needed some heavy work done or something hauled away, and on a sailor who had come home on leave once with my cousin. I thought a tattoo was a perfectly dreadful thing. And on a woman? A nice old lady?

I confided my doubts about Ruth the next day to my best friend, Gracie.

"Maybe she used to be in a circus," Gracie suggested.

"Not with just one tattoo," I said. "Still, none of the ladies we know would ever have a tattoo. It just isn't right."

"We've never seen her in church," Gracie commented. "Maybe we should invite her to come. Perhaps she needs to find Jesus." That sounded like a really good idea to me. I said I'd ask Ruth the very next time I saw her.

The next afternoon my opportunity came. Ruth gave a long look. "I have my own faith," she said quietly. "I would hope you believe in allowing all people to have their own faith."

"Everyone has the right to attend the church of his or her

choice," I stammered. "I just thought . . ."

"I will continue to worship in my own way," Ruth said firmly. "I simply do not happen to share some of the views you have."

The next day Gracie and I discussed this situation. "Ruth is always home when we go to church," Gracie pointed out. "She's home every Sunday morning too. So I think she doesn't actually go to church. Maybe she just worships God at home."

"Maybe we should slip some of those leaflets our church has into her mailbox. She might read them and decide to come to church," I said. Then I had second thoughts. "She'd blame me, though. I'm the one who asked her about going to church."

Gracie and I decided to let the matter rest for the time being. The weeks went by. Being normally curious, I tried to get a better look at the tattoo. But most of Ruth's dresses had long sleeves. I began to realize she was sensitive about her tattoo. Maybe she regretted getting it. Probably she'd been very young and made a mistake in judgment. Maybe this. Maybe that.

Then came Easter. I decided to show my belief in the risen Christ by taking Ruth a lily plant. She took the plant from me and looked very sad. I couldn't understand that.

"I understand that this is a very important time in your religion," she said, "and I thank you for giving me this plant because of your happiness at this time. I, of all people, respect the right of all people to worship openly in their own way and to follow what they believe."

I was puzzled. "I don't understand," I told her.

Ruth rolled up her sleeve. For the first time I could clearly see her tattoo. It was a number—several numbers, to be exact. Numbers? And then a feeling of horror struck me in the pit of my stomach. I was old enough to know what had been done to millions of Jewish people during the war. It had seemed too terrible to be true. I suddenly realized that my neighbor was Jewish. And that she'd been a prisoner during the recent war.

"Child, many of my family died in concentration camps,"

she told me. "How I survived is indeed a miracle. But survive I did. And I'm proud of my faith. I am as strong in my beliefs as you are in yours. It is important, my girl, that you stay firm in your faith, while allowing all others to do the same."

I took the arm with the tattoo and held it against my cheek.

"Now, you are a proud young woman, and that is good," Ruth said. "You sit down, and we will share some freshly baked cookies and some milk, you and I."

We sat across from each other at the table . . . an elderly Jewish woman and a young Christian girl, sharing . . . and I wondered why people hate, when loving gives us so much more.

OVER THE TOP

by Karl Haffner

I WONDER IF Retardo Ricardo is coming to teen camp again this summer," Ryan, the veteran counselor of Camp Kittywatchi, said to no one in particular.

"Who's that?" I questioned.

"You don't know who Retardo Ricardo is?" Ryan looked at me as if I had a banana growing out my nose. "He's about 20 years old and still comes to teen camp!"

"Ricardo, eh?"

"Well, actually," Ryan explained, "his real name is Rick Rice, but we all call him Retardo Ricardo for short."

"I beg your pardon," the girls' director, Leanne Michaels, barged in. "We don't *all* call him Retardo Ricardo. Only you and your immature buddies call him that."

Ryan's sunburn suddenly got two shades brighter as he stared at his Reeboks. "Oh, ah, hi, Leanne. I was just telling Karl about him so he'd know what to expect."

"Rick Rice is a very nice boy—uh, I mean man. He's got a couple handicaps is all."

"I didn't say he wasn't a nice guy, I just said—"

"We know what you said," Leanne snapped back. "Just cool it with the retardo stuff, would you? Poor guy's got it hard enough with the campers picking on him, let alone a counselor."

The conversation was dropped with no further thought given to Rick Rice. Camp Kittywatchi turned into an anthill of activity as the staff scurried about in preparation for a new wave of campers. The Ski Nautiques needed to be washed, the horses fed, the kitchen floor waxed—the chores seemed endless.

Hoooooonk! Hoooooonk! The air horn on the bus announced, "Ready or not, here come the campers." I watched the teens swarm out both ends of the bus.

Even though I had never seen Rick Rice, I recognized him immediately. He had a body the size of a beanpole with a head the size of a beach ball. His left shoulder drooped. His right hand twitched. His left hand clutched a ratty Teddy bear.

The teens scurried to their cabins, while Ricky stood in a daze by the bus. I approached him cautiously. "Hi, I'm Karl."

"Auuugh! Auuugh! I'm Ricky."

"Oh! Good to meet you."

"And this is Punky Brewster!" he exclaimed as he pressed the Teddy bear in my face.

"Where you from, Ricky?"

"Two plus two equals Texas."

"Can I give you a hand with your bags?"

"Auuugh!" he replied with a smile.

By the time we reached the cabin, all but one of the campers had left for supper. "Auuugh!" Ricky announced to the lone camper still unpacking.

"Hi, I'm Mike," he responded.

I gazed at Mike, hardly believing he was a teenager. His curly blond hair accented his tan. His Gold's Gym tank top highlighted his physique. He had rippling biceps and bulging triceps and massive bottomceps. He displayed such confidence as he pulled his Kidder ski from the designer ski bag.

"Hi, Mike," I said. "Welcome to the Navajos' cabin. We have the best cabin."

"Great!" Mike flashed an Ultrabrite grin as he turned toward Ricky. "What's your name?"

"Auuugh! I'm Ricky," he blurted. "If you're a bad boy, they'll make you into a girl."

We erupted in laughter. "I like your style, Ricky," Mike replied. "Let's go to supper together, what do you say?"

"Auuugh!" was the only reply.

The following day I stared in disbelief as I saw Mike and Ricky walking to mountaineering class. I wondered. Why would they let Ricky sign up for mountaineering? He'll never climb the wall.

"Good morning," I welcomed as the teens plopped in a semicircle around me. "I'm Karl, and I'll be teaching you rock rappelling. Have any of you gone rock repelling before?"

"Auuugh!" Ricky blurted out before anyone could respond. The campers erupted in giggles.

"Ricky, you have, huh?"

"Auuugh! Marshmallows make sticky eyelids!"

"OK, good," I said amidst a chorus of snickers. "Let me explain the ground rules when you're near the wall. Number one: Never attempt to climb the wall unless I am at the top of it and you are properly roped in and—"

"How tall is the wall?" a redheaded boy interrupted.

"It's 40 feet."

"Whew!" the campers sighed together.

"Number two: Always let me check the knots you tie in your rope before you climb. And number three: Choose a partner and always climb with your partner."

Mike glanced toward Ricky. "Want to be partners?" he asked.

"Auuugh," Ricky replied.

"Who wants to try climbing the wall first?" I asked.

Mike's hand shot up. "We will," he volunteered as he grabbed Ricky and dashed toward the wall. Mike climbed up the wall like a squirrel scampering up an oak tree.

"Good job," I congratulated as he dragged himself over the ledge at the top. "You've done this before, eh?"

"Oh, yeah," he replied as he looked over the edge to Ricky. "Piece of cake, Ricky. Come on up."

Ricky clutched Punky Brewster as he hugged the wall. He climbed about two feet up the wall, then froze.

All the kids stared. Nobody moved. Nobody whispered.

"Can't climb with Punky," I informed him as he clung to the wall. "Ricky, drop the Teddy bear," I hollered.

"Auuugh!"

"Ricky, drop the Teddy bear," I repeated.

Ricky twirled his head to examine how high he had climbed. When he saw he had ascended the astonishing span of two feet, he let go of the wall and collapsed on the ground with a mighty "Auuugh."

Mike bolted to Ricky's rescue. "That's OK," Mike consoled as he brushed the dirt off Ricky's back. "You got farther than I did the first time."

All week Ricky played in a sandpile near the wall while the other campers developed their skills at mountain climbing. Ricky didn't say much, just "Vroooooom, vroooooom" as he pretended Punky Brewster was a fire truck in the desert.

Much to my surprise, however, Ricky was becoming quite popular. I figured it was because Mike was always with Ricky, and the teens wanted to be around Mike. Or because of Ricky's humorous (albeit nonsensical) one-liners. For whatever reason, the campers seemed to enjoy having Ricky around.

It wasn't until Friday that someone suggested Ricky try climbing the wall again. Ricky looked up from the sandpile and uttered, "Auuugh."

Mike crouched on his knees in the sand next to Ricky. "What do you say, Ricky? Give the wall one more shot."

"Auuugh. I dunno."

"C'mon, Ricky, you can do it."

"But the wall's soooooo big."

"Nothing you can't do," Mike encouraged.

"Opossums go to the road to die. Auuugh." Ricky's one-liners seemed most frequent whenever he got nervous.

"C'mon, Ricky, you can do it!" Mike grabbed his arm and guided him toward the wall.

The other campers crowded around Ricky. "Riiiii-*cky*! Riiiii-*cky*! Riiiii-*cky*!" they chanted as if they were filming a Sylvester Stallone movie.

"I dunno if I can . . ."

No one heard Ricky's attempt to protest. Before Ricky could say Punky, he was two feet up the wall.

"You're almost there; only 38 feet to go," Mike shouted.

"Go, Ricky!" screamed a girl in the back.

Ricky crawled upward. His footing unsure. His hands quivering faster than the wings of a hummingbird on steroids. Nonetheless, he inched upward.

"C'mon, Ricky!" I squealed from the ledge on top. "You can do it."

After climbing about 15 feet, Ricky stopped to rate his progress. "Auuugh! Auuugh!" he shrieked as he realized he was too high to bail out easily.

"I've got you roped in, Ricky. It won't hurt if you fall. Keep climbing!" I shouted from the top.

Ricky staggered upward. Concentration burned in his eyes.

"Go Ricky, you can do it! Yeeeeehaaaawooooo, Ricky!" The campers screamed. There was so much chaos some of the campers and staff from the horse corral came to see what the racket was all about. I glanced at the new spectators. I noticed even Ryan had dropped in to cheer Ricky the mountain climber.

With only eight feet left in his ascent, Ricky panicked. He froze. Motionless. Petrified.

Grabbing Punky Brewster from the sandpile, Mike raced up the stairs to the platform at the top. Holding Punky Brewster over the edge, Mike hollered, "Come on up here; Punky's waiting for you!"

With his eyes fixed on Punky, Ricky scaled the homeward stretch with the grace of Spiderman. As we dragged Ricky onto the platform, the kids exploded in pandemonium.

Hugging Punky, all Ricky could say was "Auuugh!"

LETTER TO NORMA JEAN

by Enola Fargusson

THE HEADLINES ON the morning paper seemed to leap out at me. Tears trickling down my cheeks, I reached into my writing drawer, took out a half-finished letter, and dropped it into the wastebasket. No need to mail it now.

"I'm sorry, Norma Jean," I whispered. "I didn't know."

The golden girl, rich, famous, beautiful, adored by millions, was dead. She had committed suicide.

My mind drifted back over the years. We were both 14 the summer we spent together. Mother was sick a lot that year. Just before school was out, she'd had an operation and her recovery was slow. Mrs. Enright, a neighbor, had recommended Grace, a friend of hers, to look after our house and do the shopping for us.

At first, Grace didn't mention Norma Jean. In fact, we first heard about her when Mrs. Enright asked her one afternoon how Norma Jean was spending the summer.

"She hoped to get a job," Grace said. "Since she couldn't find one, she's just hanging around our apartment, reading and listening to the radio."

"Who's Norma Jean?" I asked.

"She's the daughter of a friend," Grace explained. "Her

mother is in a mental institution and she has no other relatives, so I look after her."

"Bring her along with you," Mother suggested.

"I'll pay her to help with my housework in the mornings," Mrs. Enright put in. "Then the two girls can spend the afternoons together."

So it was decided, and with mixed emotions I waited for Norma Jean to come on the scene. On the one hand, I was glad for the companionship, since most of my friends were gone for the summer. But on the other hand, there was the religious difference.

You see, I had recently started attending a Seventh-day Adventist church. We had distant relatives who were Adventists, and everything was going along all right until Mrs. Enright and Grace stepped in. They were Christian Scientists, and Mother had begun studying with them.

Mother's newfound Adventist faith was shaky, but she wasn't ready to give it up yet. So, while she urged me to read Christian Science literature, she didn't forbid me to go to church on Sabbath.

I was to discover that the two religions were quite opposite. While Adventists believe that sin and sickness are the result of Satan's rebellion against God, Christian Scientists believe they are the result of wrong thoughts. Evil exists in men's minds, they claim, and if people can eradicate these thoughts, sin and sickness will evaporate from the earth.

I was sure Mrs. Enright and Grace wanted Norma Jean to influence me toward Christian Science.

"That can work two ways," I decided. "I'll influence her instead." How I wish I had!

Norma Jean and I soon found we had a lot in common. She was just a little taller than I. We both had dark hair and freckles, and the complexion that goes with them. We had the same taste in clothes, in music, and in reading. Norma Jean's mother and Grace had been in the motion-picture business, the field my stepfather was in. Thus we knew some of the same people. She never knew her father, and mine had died when I was very young.

But there were also differences. Whereas I had loving grandparents and many aunts, uncles, and cousins, she had only her mother, who had been institutionalized when Norma Jean was 2. I had an attractive, well-furnished room of my own, while Norma Jean was never sure whether she would have a home or not.

Shortly after stepping in to act as her guardian, Grace had married Doc Goddard, a man whose occupation could best be described as a promoter. Doc was a visionary. He had ideas— some good, some bad. When he put together a profitable venture, Grace and Norma Jean lived well. When his deals fell through and he ended up broke, Grace would appeal to the County Welfare Department, and Norma Jean would end up in a foster home.

At the moment, Doc was barely making ends meet. He was working on an out-of-town business deal that would soon provide them with a comfortable living. In the meantime, they lived in a tiny apartment. When Doc joined them for the weekends, Norma Jean slept on the couch in the living room.

Although her life was often bleak, Norma Jean had a happy disposition. We talked and laughed together, went for walks, played games, and sometimes spent the afternoons reading.

One afternoon, when she was relating a bad experience she'd had in a foster home, I finally got the chance I was waiting for.

"Whatever happens," I told her, "Jesus loves you."

"I know," she replied. "If it weren't for what I've learned in my church, I don't think I'd be able to survive."

I knew I should say more. The trouble was, I couldn't think what. I'd been going to church only a few months. I'd been studying the Bible, reading *Steps to Christ*, and keeping the Morning Watch, but I wondered whether I knew enough to teach someone else.

Just tell her what Jesus means to you, an inner voice urged.

We've got the rest of the summer, I argued. *Probably longer. After Doc's deal goes through, they're going to buy a house near here, so we'll be attending the same school. There's no hurry.*

I went on studying and praying and thinking about what I would tell Norma Jean later, when the time was right and I was smarter. And suddenly, time ran out.

"Guess what?" Mother said one afternoon when she and Grace returned from the doctor's office. "Dr. Immerman says I can do my own work now."

Grace was smiling too.

"I stopped by our apartment and there was a letter from Doc," she told Norma Jean. "He's about to close his business deal and wants us to join him. Since we're not needed here, we can leave in the morning."

"So soon!" I cried.

"Don't worry," Grace assured me. "We'll be back before school begins." But they weren't. Instead, Doc bought a house in a neighboring town.

I saw Norma Jean once in a while when Grace visited Mrs. Enright and brought her along, but Mother had lost interest in Christian Science, so even these visits were short.

Norma Jean had her own room now, and Doc was making enough money so that she would never have to go to another foster home. Although I was happy for her, I still wanted to tell her about the Jesus I knew. But I couldn't find a way to fit Him in our brief conversations.

Two years had gone, but then Grace phoned Mother one afternoon.

"Norma Jean is married," Mother told me afterward.

"She's too young," I protested. "She's only 16."

"It was probably Grace's idea," Mother replied. "She feels it's best for Norma Jean. At least she'll have someone to look after her."

"Who'd she marry?" I asked.

"A neighbor in his late 20s," Mother said. "He has his own home and can support her comfortably on his policeman's salary."

I felt sorry for Norma Jean, but I was busy and gradually

pushed her to the back of my mind. I graduated from school, got a job, married and had a family. For a while, I stopped going to church, but God didn't give up on me. I came back to Him, was baptized, and, with church activities, found myself busier than ever.

One day I ran into Mrs. Enright on a street corner. I hadn't seen her for several years, so I told her about my family, and she brought me up-to-date on hers.

"Do you ever hear from Norma Jean?" I asked.

"I don't believe those terrible things they say about her, do you?" she burst out indignantly.

"What things?" I asked, puzzled.

"Don't you know?" She seemed surprised. "Norma Jean is Marilyn Monroe, the movie star."

I was stunned. Mr. Enright drove up just then, so I waved goodbye.

Could Mrs. Enright be losing her mind? I wondered. But I bought a magazine that had Marilyn Monroe's picture on the cover and took it home. There under a bright light, I mentally stripped off the layers of theatrical makeup and darkened her now-blonde hair. Sure enough, it was really Norma Jean.

My first reaction was to write her a letter. Then I laughed at myself. Movie stars, I knew, receive so much mail they can't possibly handle it themselves. They hire entire staffs to take care of such correspondence.

So again I put Norma Jean out of my mind. Anyway, what could I say to her now? She had everything.

Oh, I read about her. Newspapers and magazines were full of her comings and goings, her romances, her marriages and divorces, travels, and theatrical successes.

One day I heard that Marilyn Monroe had moved back to Hollywood from New York.

Write her, an inner voice urged.

"What can I say to her, Lord?" I wailed. "She has everything."

She doesn't have Me, the voice persisted. *Tell her what*

I've done for you.

So I got out my best stationery, addressed an envelope, and began writing. But halfway through, I got cold feet.

Would she even see the letter? Or would a secretary or a maid throw it away?

I read over what I'd written.

Needs work, I decided, tossing it into a drawer. *I'm too tired tonight. I'll finish it tomorrow.*

I prayed about it. I threw away the letter I'd begun, and started over. Every few days I went through the same routine, scratching out words and phrases, discarding it, beginning again.

And then the headlines.

MARILYN MONROE COMMITS SUICIDE.

"I'm sorry, God. I'm sorry, Norma Jean."

Would she have listened? I'll never know. At least I could have tried. If I'd only stopped worrying enough to let God lead the way.

Maybe, just maybe, the girl who had everything—except God—might have lived.

ALWAYS

by Charles Mills

PIECE OF CAKE," Steve's boss, Morgan Hetrick, said cheerfully. "Just drive the load of cocaine from Florida to California." The man leaned forward a little. "And don't worry—you'll be the only one on the road who'll know what's hiding under the back seat." He grinned mischievously. "But I wouldn't break any speed limits if I were you!"

Morgan tilted his head back and laughed long and loud, his mirth echoing across the quiet waters by Fort Lauderdale. People in the harbor restaurant turned and smiled, wondering what delightful joke the man had just heard.

Steve Arrington knew this was no joke. One misstep, and lives would be at risk—his especially. To make matters worse, a longtime friend had decided to go along for the ride.

"So we deliver a car to California." Sam's enthusiasm seemed boundless. "Big deal."

"There are things going down you don't understand," Steve warned. "Trust me. You don't want to go with me on this trip."

Sam looked first one way and then the other. "You mean about what's in the car? Under the back seat?"

Steve paled. "How—?"

"Morgan called," his friend said matter-of-factly. "Offered me five grand to ride shotgun for you."

"He *what?*"

"Yeah, so cool it," Sam grinned. "I'm not about to pass up

a sweet deal like this. I'm in for the long haul. Let's quit all this yakkity-yak and hit the road . . . partner!"

Steve felt suddenly sick inside. Sam was young and innocent, a friend he'd known for a long time. A surfing buddy. The most dangerous thing they'd ever done together was attack the big waves off the California coast. Now, because of his bad choices, Steve was about to drag good-natured Sam into a life of crime.

They drove for three days. By the time they arrived in Los Angeles, Steve had made a decision. This would be the last job he'd do for Morgan. He'd get out of the organization one way or another.

"So where's the car?" his boss asked, a slight hesitation in his voice.

"I parked it, man," Steve said firmly. "I'm out of this business. Do you understand me?"

Morgan looked as tired as he sounded. "Just tell me where the car is."

"I parked it in front of the Skyways Restaurant at the Van Nuys Airport."

"You just left it there—*unattended?*" Morgan shouted. "What! Are you *crazy?*"

"Remember? I told you I *quit!*"

"Steve!" Morgan tried to control his emotions. "You can't just quit. We're dealing with some heavy dudes here. If you don't hand over that cocaine, we'll end up in a couple of garbage bags. Do you hear me?" The man paused, then lifted his finger. "Don't move. I'll be right back."

Morgan hurried from the motel room and soon returned with two unpleasant-looking men. "Take these guys to the car, Steve. Then we'll decide what to do."

"OK," Steve agreed. "But Sam doesn't go along. You got that?"

"Yeah, yeah. Leave the kid behind."

Arriving at the Van Nuys Airport restaurant, Steve showed his two new companions where the car was parked. They gathered up some of the cocaine from under the seat and taste-tested it to make sure it was real.

Then the unexpected happened. Suddenly the car was surrounded by gun-toting men shouting instructions and throwing Steve to the ground. With heart-stopping swiftness the driver who'd decided to abandon his life of crime understood. The two men Morgan had been dealing with were undercover cops working for the Drug Enforcement Administration. Steve's worst nightmare had just become a reality. He'd been caught smuggling cocaine.

"You're under arrest, dirtbag," an agent sneered, gun pointed with deadly precision at his victim. "I guess this isn't the best day of your life, is it, creep?"

Steve's stomach churned as he fought off waves of fear-induced nausea. *At least mobsters aren't going to slit my throat*, he thought to himself.

Turning to the officer who was holding the gun against his temple, Steve said quietly, "Actually, I think it *is* the best day of my life."

The agent looked surprised, but Steve knew the meaning hiding behind his strange response. One terrifying part of his life was over. The law had finally caught up with him, trapping him in his own wrong choices.

Now another life was about to begin. From where he was standing, surrounded by a dozen federal agents, the future held little promise.

Later, riding in the police van toward that uncertain future, Steve Arrington had time to review his past. How quickly his wrong decisions had affected his life and the lives of others. He thought of the always-cheerful Sam, of his mother and family and friends, who'd learn about the arrest.

And what was God thinking right about now? Steve had considered himself a Christian for as long as he could remember. He'd known there was a Higher Power looking down on this earth, watching, judging. Would God now abandon him for good? Had he made one too many mistakes?

The answers to those questions refused to surface in his mind as the speeding van swayed and rumbled through the streets of Los Angeles. All he knew sitting there, hands and ankles cuffed securely, was that he was about to pay for his mistakes, and the cost would be terrible.

* * *

The foul smell of stale cigarette smoke and unwashed bodies filled the prisoner's nostrils. Steve shook his head as if trying to clear the odor, as well as the thoughts running through his mind.

"Five years," the judge had announced, bringing his gavel down hard against his desk.

So this is it, Steve thought to himself, trying to keep warm under the thin prison blanket he'd found waiting for him at the foot of his badly stained mattress. Overhead he felt his roommate's considerable bulk shift position on the top bunk.

The days had turned into months after his arrest at Van Nuys Airport. Now the waiting was over. The trial had come and gone; it was time to pay the price for the decisions he'd made.

Steve closed his eyes. How quickly those bad choices had turned on him, spun him around, left him out of control of his life. Tears welled up in the man's eyes—not just tears of sorrow, but of understanding. He'd turned his back on what was right, what was lawful. The judge had been fair, very fair. Breaking the law demanded punishment, even though the lawbreaker was trying to change his ways. No matter the good intentions; damage had already been done. Steve knew that, and he accepted his fate.

But now, in the relative silence of his lonely prison cell, the full wages of his sins were being delivered with an impact he'd never known was possible. Visions of family members, close friends, and the smiles of people he'd worked with seemed like nothing more than faded pictures hanging on the moldy walls of the cell. He couldn't hear their voices anymore, even when he tried to remember how they sounded.

His world had become so small, so violent, so hopeless. Days were bad enough, filled with evil men with evil intentions. But the nights—how they weighed on him, pressing him down against the bare springs of his filthy mattress.

Steve slipped from the bunk, his knees striking the cold stone floor with a soft thud. His guilt felt like hands gripping his throat and squeezing his lungs, making it harder and harder to breathe.

"God," he whispered, letting the full agony in his heart lift the word with unfathomable sorrow. "O, God! Have You left me too? Have You turned Your back on me?"

Glancing upward, he agonized a heartfelt plea. "Are You . . . are You there for me?"

Through the silence came an instant reply. It wasn't delivered out loud. No voice spoke. But suddenly one word filled the prisoner's heart and mind. In his darkest hour Steve knew he'd heard God's response to his question. The answer was— "Always."

The man buried his face in his hands. From this moment forward, no matter what the future held, he'd not have to face it alone. Despair had taken flight, leaving in its place the life-lifting power of hope.

Epilogue: Steve Arrington was released after serving four years in prison. He later became the chief expedition diver for the Cousteau Society. More recently he has been involved in writing about his experiences and speaking out against substance abuse.

SONG IN THE NIGHT

by Rosemary Peyton

MELODY TOSSED THE sheet aside and slid out of bed. The wooden floor felt warm against her bare feet as she padded through the next room where her younger sisters slept. Quickly, quietly, in case Mama should be awake and send her back to bed, she tiptoed across the hall.

The dining room door swung open with a creak, and a tell-tale board popped, shattering the stillness. Melody's breath caught in her throat. Leaning against the doorframe, the teenager stared at the empty rocking chair in its place by the windows. Summer moonlight spilled over it like a benediction.

"Of course he's not here," she whispered. "It was a dream." Blinking back sudden hot tears, Melly stumbled toward her room.

Pausing beside 4-year-old Cammy's bed, she knelt and buried her face in the little girl's long curls. Cammy clutched her comforter, "Kunky."

Ann, her other sister, stirred and raised herself up onto one elbow.

"What's wrong?" she demanded sharply. But it was only fear that made Annie so difficult lately.

"Ssh . . . nothing. Just thought I heard Cammy," Melody

lied. "Must've been the cat or something. Go back to sleep." Aware of Ann's blue-gray eyes boring into her back, she rose and crossed through the wide arched doorway that divided her tiny room from their larger one.

Melly crawled back onto her bed and let her mind drift with the night sounds that floated in through the open windows. That was the one thing this house they were renting had going for it, lots of big windows. And they were surrounded by lawns and fields and trees as though they lived far out in the country, yet were within walking distance of town.

Sometimes one of the landlord's cows broke out of the pasture, and Cammy and Dog, their glossy-black dachshund, would hightail it, screaming and yelping, to the house. Then nothing would do until Daddy cuddled her on his lap in the rocker. He'd sing to her, pretending not to know that Melody sat out in the hall listening. Daddy's sweet, clear tenor comforted his daughters and lulled the youngest to sleep.

When Cammy nodded off, her head supported against his thin, cobalt-burned chest, he'd close the impromptu concert with his favorite hymn, "Rock of Ages." Melody would join in, and they'd sing it to the end:

"While I draw this fleeting breath,
When mine eyes shall close in death,
When I soar to worlds unknown,
See Thee on Thy judgment throne,
Rock of Ages, cleft for me,
Let me hide myself in Thee."

Mr. Bradman sat in his rocker and sang also when the pain jarred him awake in the middle of the night. Melody often slipped through the darkness to keep him company, but always he reassured her, "I'm all right; go back to bed, sweetheart. You need your rest. It's all right."

It was that song that had beckoned her into the dining room a few minutes before. She'd heard Daddy singing it, seen him rocking, a big smile on his face—his healthy tanned face. He had some flesh on his bones, too, and his stomach wasn't swollen with the fluid that the doctors couldn't seem to drain off fast enough.

"Dummy," she chided herself, "it was only a dream." Suddenly a wonderful thought took root in her mind. Perhaps it was a dream—sent from God! Maybe He was trying to tell her that Daddy, who this very moment lay in the Marshall Hospital, was going to get well and come home to them. That had to be it! Joy flushed her cheeks and made her brown eyes dance. Too excited to lie still, she sat up and hugged her gangly legs, breathing a simple prayer: "Thank You, Jesus."

Ann's gentle snore told her that the girl had fallen asleep. With pounding heart Melly swung her legs over the side of the bed once more and squatted on the floor, cautiously pulling open a dresser drawer. From its hiding place she removed a heart-shaped pink plastic box. Grabbing a flashlight off the bedside table, she sat down and unlocked her treasure. A pink-and-gold five-year diary lay among dried corsages, notes, and a letter that Daddy had written to her before his family joined him in Texas two years ago. Melody had refused to mention his illness in her diary. The terrible word *cancer* was one she couldn't bring herself to write. Now she scrawled on one entire page, "Daddy's been sick, but he's going to be all right."

Heavy-eyed but happier than she'd been in a long time, Melly clicked off the flashlight and hopped back into bed.

Next morning she didn't say anything about the marvelous secret that the Lord had revealed to her. When Daddy began to get better, then she would tell her family about the dream.

After Mrs. Bradman left for the hospital, Ann slammed out of the house and climbed far up into the apple tree that shaded their backyard. Melody let her go without a word. Pastor Collins would be picking Grandma up at the Shreveport Airfield soon. Once she arrived, everything would be fine. Grandmother Van Ralte was scarcely five feet tall, but she had a glint in her black eyes that dared anyone to disobey, and Ann adored her. Melody's heart was so light that she settled down on the couch with Cammy and read the tyke's favorite story, "The Little Engine That Could," a couple times without being asked.

As they were hollering, "I think I can, I think I can!" tires crunched up the driveway. Cammy wriggled off the couch, squealing with delight.

"Melly, Grandma's here. Hurry!" They dashed hand in hand across the porch and down the steps. Cammy threw her arms around Grandma's hips as Ann loped around the corner of the brownstone house. She looked like a little gypsy in her wrinkled shorts set, black hair falling into her face. Brother Collins, a Southern Baptist minister who had befriended them, lifted the elderly lady's bags out of his car and carried them inside while she took stock of her youngest daughter's children.

"How are my girls?"

"We're all fine, Grandma." Melly acted as spokesperson.

"Ann, Cammy, have you been minding your sister?"

They nodded solemnly, chorusing, "Yes'm," but Ann cast a furtive glance at Melody.

"They've been real good, Grandma."

"I'm glad to hear it." Mrs. Van Ralte smiled, brushing Ann's bangs out of her yes. "Melody, honey," she continued, as the minister rejoined them, "please keep Pastor Collins company while Ann and I get lunch on the table. Cammy, come tell Grandmother what you've been up to."

"Is this your new car?" Melody asked the silver-haired man.

"Would you like to take me for a ride?" he teased, a grin splitting his face. He knew the answer to that! His young friend had just completed driver's ed and jumped at every opportunity to get behind the wheel.

"Really? I'll go check with Grandma!" she exclaimed, running into the house. In no time they were on their way.

The summer breeze carried the tangy scent of honeysuckle and east Texas wildflowers into the open automobile. To Melly, the sky had never looked so blue, nor the clouds as whipped-cream-thick and fluffy. The sun washed the world clean and bright as it climbed higher in the heaves.

"Can you keep a secret?" Melody asked after a while.

"What do you think?"

"Sure, you can." Melody slowed the car and pulled into the dusty yard of a deserted barbecue stand. She circled around and parked in the shade of an old pine tree. "This is a great car."

"Thank you. The Lord is good."

"I know it. He's going to make my daddy well." A brilliant red cardinal played hide-and-seek with his mate in the bushes across the road. Silence greeted her announcement. Sensing the pastor's steady blue eyes upon her, Melody looked at him. Compassion and sorrow mingled in his expression.

"He is," she repeated adamantly. "Last night He gave me a sign, a promise, Daddy's not going to die."

"That's . . . that's wonderful." He chose his words carefully. "You have a pure simple faith, Melly. God can use people who have that kind of trust in Him. What impressed you to believe He has a miracle in store for Carl?"

"I don't know," she blushed, avoiding his gaze. "Just something. You know . . ." Somehow she couldn't bring herself to tell him about her dream.

"Melly, the devil enjoys hurting God's children. And God, because He is our loving Father, longs to reach down and undo all the evil and suffering that the enemy causes."

"Then why doesn't He?" she snapped.

"Honey, sometimes we must come to the place, as did Job, where we can say, 'Though He slay me, yet will I trust in Him.' Job mistakenly believed that God was responsible for his misery, but he still lifted up his heart to the Lord in faith and love. Carl has come to that place, Melly. Whether God heals him or not, your daddy has placed himself and his family in the care of those nail-scarred hands."

Melody watched a buzzard glide overhead. A cold shiver prickled down her spine in spite of the noonday heat. Composing herself, she flashed the minister a polite smile that didn't quite reach her eyes.

"I understand what you're saying. Thank you." But she didn't, and the kindhearted man knew it and tried to draw her out again. But before he'd spoken two words, the engine roared to life.

"We'd better head back. Grandma'll have lunch ready. I'm starved!"

A few days later Mr. Bradman came home. Several of his brothers drove from Mississippi to visit, sat silently pressing crisp bills into his reluctant hand in parting. They were tall, reticent men, bound by a love they couldn't speak. Not long after that, their Arkansas relatives caravanned down, taking Grandma back with them when they left.

Summer freedom came to an end as August slipped into September and school began. Melly and Ann were never sure when Daddy kissed them Goodbye in the morning that he'd be there to greet them when they got off the school bus in the afternoon. And he no longer sang during the endless, pain-wracked nights. The rocking chair wailed a mournful solo until he grew too weak to leave the rented hospital bed without assistance.

Melly tried to rekindle the hope that had flamed up in her heart, but it was no match against autumn's chill. Each time they took Daddy back to the hospital, Pastor Collins' words jabbed a bony finger in her face.

One Saturday morning in late October, Mama shook Melody awake while it was still dark.

"Daddy's had a rough night, sugar. You get your sisters up and help Cammy dress and pack. We'll spend the weekend together in Marshall with Uncle Charlie and Aunt Bea." She referred to their good friends the Cooks. "And then . . . then I think it'd be best if you two big girls accept the Blevins' offer to stay with them for a while. I'm depending on you to help Ann, understand, Melly?"

Melly felt as though ice water had been dashed in her face. Help Ann? How could she help Ann when she didn't understand herself? They'd discussed the possibility of a separation, but she had never dreamed it would happen so soon. At last she found her voice. "That's OK, Mama. We'll do fine."

Soon the Bradmans were ready to leave for the hospital.

Melody parted the bedroom curtains and peered out at the cold, gray dawn. Ann huddled in the car, her face pressed against a frosty window. What was she thinking? Remembering Cammy's motion-sickness medicine in the kitchen, the older girl crossed the hall and found the bottle, stuffing it into her coat pocket. As she cut through the dining room, her father shuffled to the hall door. He paused on the threshold, exhausted by the effort of walking from his bedroom. When he saw Melody, he held out his arms. She ran to him and buried her face in his shirt, and he rested his sunken cheek against the top of her curly brown head. For one golden moment, time seemed suspended. Then Mama appeared with Daddy's coat, Cammy at her heels. Melly stooped down and buttoned her sister's wraps.

"I'll read to you at the hospital, and later Uncle Charlie and Aunt Bea will come and take us to their house," she chattered aimlessly.

At the hospital they went through the familiar ritual at the admissions desk. The nurses knew them all by name. Mama looked so tired, but she held herself erect. Melly stared at the round clock on the wall to keep from crying. Across the room, Ann slouched on a yellow vinyl couch, Cammy's head nestled in her lap.

On Sunday evening the Blevins drove over to see Mr. Bradman and pick Melody and Ann up. They seemed happy to have two extra children and a dog to look after. If they found the task burdensome at all, they were too kind to let on as the weeks sped by. Melly had to admit that it was a relief just to be a kid and let someone else take care of things for a while. Even though God had failed them, she reasoned, they had good friends like the Blevins and Cooks to depend upon.

The weeks sped by. Every Friday evening Uncle Charlie and Aunt Bea took them to Marshall to be with their father, mother, and baby sister. One Friday the girls came in from school to find Uncle Charlie's blue car already parked in the driveway. The adults stopped talking when the youngsters stepped through the back door. Small, wiry Uncle Charlie jumped up and wrapped his best friend's children in a bear hug.

"Get your gear, young'uns. Auntie Bea's expecting us at the flower shop." They hurried to obey. When they were ready, Mrs. Blevins and her boys walked them out to the car and squeezed them goodbye. During the short trip Uncle Charlie told stories about his childhood in Oregon even though he knew they weren't listening. Aunt Bea was waiting on the sidewalk when they pulled up to the curb.

"We timed that perfectly, didn't we?" she asked brightly, settling her little round self into the car. "The day's so sunny and crisp that I couldn't stand being cooped up inside that stuffy shop! Fall's just painted herself up like an aging debutante this year!" She laughed a trifle weakly, and patted Ann's knee.

They went immediately to the hospital. The feeling of dread gnawing at Melly's stomach turned to horror when she saw her father. He had grown so much worse since they'd seen him the week before. Dark shadows circled his gentle gray eyes, and lines of pain cut sharp paths alongside his mouth.

Why, God, why? she cried silently, as Ann and she hung over the rails of his bed, one on either side. They talked about unimportant things, and held his hands. Melly thought of all the times she'd sat in church as a child playing with those long, slender fingers, and how secure she'd felt with her tiny hand tucked into his large one as she'd walked into the great unknown of first grade. And now he had to walk into another unknown, and she couldn't go with him. Oh, *why?*

"Charlie?" Mr. Bradman called softly.

"I'm here, Carl."

"Lift Cammy up here, will you?"

"Sure, Carl." Uncle Charlie's voice sounded funny. For a long time Daddy stroked his baby girl's silky hair.

"OK, Charlie," he whispered at last.

"Time to go, girls." Aunt Bea managed a lopsided smile. They each strained over the metal railings and planted kisses on Daddy's ashen cheeks. A strand of black hair curled over his damp forehead. Melly wanted to remember everything.

"I love you, Daddy," she croaked.

"I love you, sweetheart . . . it'll be all right," he promised. In the morning he was gone.

At the funeral Mrs. Cornelius stood in the second-story balcony of the church and sang "Rock of Ages." Outside the stained-glass windows, the icy November wind moaned in accompaniment. Pastor Collins caught Melly's eye. She quickly looked away, but his words echoed in her mind. And to her surprise, instead of a sharp bony finger, she felt the tender caress of a long slender one against her face. She stared at Daddy in his familiar black suit. His face was smooth, peaceful; the shadows faded. With a trembling smile on her lips she looked back at the pastor as if to say, "It'll be all right."

NARROW
ESCAPES

4

KIDNAPPED!

by Goldie Down

IT WAS A good feeling. Prem lay back idly on his rope bed and thought about his morning's work.

He had met with good success in his bookselling, and a pocketful of money witnessed to all the orders he had taken.

Prem yawned widely and stretched his arms above his head. It was early afternoon—siesta time—and there was no use calling on people at this hour. They would be more interested in sleep at this time of day than in buying books.

Sleep. He could do with some himself. He hadn't been feeling too well lately. Maybe an afternoon off wouldn't hurt.

Prem turned over on his side and shut his eyes, but just before his eyelids closed he glimpsed the date on the gaudy calendar hanging on the wall. "Wednesday, February 12."

Instantly Prem was wide awake and staring at the calendar again. "Wednesday, February 12, 1969."

He began counting aloud to himself. My, what a lot there was to do and how little time to do it in. Four months—only four months, and he had to earn a college scholarship plus as much extra money as possible. There was no one to help him; he had to rely on himself and God.

"In that case"—Prem slowly sat up and swung his feet over the side of the bed—"I have no time for sleeping the daylight hours away. I'd better get up and get going!"

All the time Prem was combing his hair and getting his books together, he was thinking hard. It would be no use calling on people in Rewa at this hour; they were resting and would be angry at being disturbed. But Chutterpur was in his territory too, and he had planned to go there one day. Today was as good as any other. If he took an express bus, he could reach there about 4:00 p.m., sell books at the school he had in mind, and then get a bus back to Rewa before dark.

The bus jolted and rocked the long miles to Chutterpur, and the hot breeze it stirred up as it swayed along was far from pleasant.

When the bus finally stopped, Prem started quickly toward the school address. He was certain he would make a sale there, and he did. It was too late in the day to go searching for other prospects: he would return to Chutterpur some other time and cover the town thoroughly.

Prem headed back toward the bus station. As he walked along he heard a car coming down the road behind him. He stepped well over to the side, but to his surprise the car stopped when it drew abreast of him and a man alighted and came forward.

"Where are you going?" the man asked.

"I am returning to Rewa," Prem answered politely, though he was mystified by the man's action. He racked his brain to remember whether he had ever see him before. Was it possible he had met him when he was selling books somewhere?

"My name is Nand Kishore," the man said as if in answer to Prem's thoughts. "I come from Jabalpur. What is your name?"

"My name is Prem Chand," Prem replied.

"Fine, Prem. Come along in the car with us, and we'll give you a lift as far as Rewa."

Prem did not hesitate for a moment. "No, thank you," he said politely. "I'll go by bus. I have a return ticket."

All the stories Prem had heard about bandits and kidnappers rushed into his mind, and now he knew for certain he had never seen this man before.

"Get into the car!"

Another man had quietly stepped up behind Prem. He grabbed the boy's bag, and the two men pushed the frightened youth roughly into the back seat!

As the car gathered speed, Prem sank back trembling. This was the first time he had ever been to Chutterpur, and the area was strange to him. He didn't know whether to try shouting for help or doing something else. He had heard that some districts in this country were completely lawless and the whole community lived by theft and plunder and often murder. Had he unknowingly come to such a place? Would these men rob and kill him? Should he try to open the door and jump out?

Prem's racing thoughts kept time with his churning stomach. For several days past he had felt sick, and now this alarming experience had him so terrified he almost lost consciousness. He didn't think of praying for help; his mind was too numbed by fear to think of anything but the dreadful death that awaited him at the hands of these terrible men.

After driving for a long time, the men in the car pulled up at a lonely spot and bundled Prem out and hurried him into an empty house. He was pushed into a small room and left alone for what seemed to him like an hour or more.

What are those men doing? Prem wondered. *Probably they are searching my bag in the hope of finding valuables! When they find it contains nothing but books they will be so angry they will surely kill me.*

Prem crouched on the floor of the empty room and wondered what was going to happen next.

Suddenly the door was flung open and three men entered. These were different men, not the two who had carried him off in the car from Chutterper.

"Give us your money," demanded the first man, towering over Prem.

Prem took out his money purse. He knew that it contained 200 rupees, his earnings for several weeks. (He never dared to leave his purse in his lodgings, because thieving was so common. It was far safer to keep the whole sum with him until he could deposit it.)

"Is that all you've got?" The man had opened the purse,

and now he looked at Prem threateningly. "Come on, don't try to hide any. Give us all the money you have, or we'll kill you and take it."

With six hard black eyes glowering at him, Prem turned out all his pockets and found two more small coins, which together were worth only about a penny. He held them out.

"That is all I have," he said. "You can search me if you like. I have nothing more."

The men left the room angrily, and for 10 minutes more Prem was alone with his agonized thoughts.

Abruptly the men returned. Two of them yanked Prem to his feet and tied a cloth over his face. He did not struggle; he knew it was no use. He would have no chance with three men against him.

Roughly the men pushed him out of the house and into a jeep. *This is the end*, Prem thought. *They'll drive to some deserted spot, stab me, and throw my body into a river.*

The minutes seemed to drag into hours as the trembling boy awaited his doom. He thought of his mother and his young brother at home. They would miss him greatly. Maybe his body would never be found. Maybe his mother would never know what happened to him.

Prem's tortured thoughts were interrupted by the changing sound of the wheels' steady hum. The jeep was slowing down.

Without warning strong arms grabbed Prem and threw him from the slowly moving vehicle like a sack of wheat. He lay without moving until the sound of the departing jeep faded into the distance. He had no idea where he was. He had not been able to see a thing since leaving the empty house.

Prem sat up and struggled to untie the cloth that was bound about his head. He heard approaching footsteps, and hope stirred in his heart.

"Help me!" he called in a muffled voice. "Help me get this cloth off my head!"

The footsteps stopped, and someone began tugging at the knots.

"Whatever has happened to you?" a voice asked. "Who tied

you up like this? Are you hurt?"

"I don't know. I'm bruised all over, but I'm still alive!" As the stranger helped him to his feet, he asked, "Where am I?"

"We are on the outskirts of Rewa," the kind stranger told him. "They robbed you, eh? There is too much of that sort of thing going on. But they will be caught," he prophesied darkly. "Now, tell me where you live, and I will help you get home."

"I am staying right here in Rewa, with P. L. Brown on Inder Road," Prem said.

His legs felt like jelly, and his stomach still churned. His head felt 10 sizes too large for his body. Without help he could never have walked the distance to his lodgings.

After his good Samaritan had left him safely at the door of his house, Prem began to relax a little. Once more he sank onto his rope bed. A lot had happened since the last time he lay on that bed! Except for the goodness of God he would now be a miserable corpse flung into some faraway ditch.

He shuddered. How merciful God was to have saved his life.

"Thank You, God," he murmured aloud. "Thank You for saving me, even when I was so scared that I forgot to pray."

THE STORY OF DESMOND T. DOSS

by Charles Mills

HEY, look at the preacher!" A sarcastic voice shouted across the wide, wooden, army barracks at Fort Jackson, South Carolina.

Company D's new recruits turned and stared at a young, slender figure kneeling beside a low bunk by the window. The soldier's mouth moved silently as he prayed.

"He's probably asking God to get him out of the Army!" another called. Laughter erupted from the crowd of men in green fatigues.

Suddenly a heavy Army boot sailed over the praying man's bunk and smashed into a metal cabinet standing against the wall.

More shoes arched through the air, accompanied by a foul stream of mocking remarks. The hands folded in prayer trembled slightly.

The mournful strains of taps quieted the assault as men flopped into bed and the barracks settled into silence. The lonely recruit with the wavy brown hair whispered an emotional amen and slipped under the thin, olive-drab blanket. Private Desmond T. Doss's first day in the United States Army, 77th Infantry Division, had ended. The year was 1942.

Returning from breakfast the next morning, Doss felt a

heavy hand on his shoulder. An angry-voiced soldier spat words into his face. "Listen, holy Jesus, when we go into combat you're not comin' back alive. You wanna know why?"

The young recruit stared back unflinchingly into the squinting eyes. "'Cause if the Japs don't kill you, *I will!*" The man turned and stormed away.

Desmond Doss was a Seventh-day Adventist—had been all his young life. He'd grown up on Bible stories of men and women who'd stood up for their religious beliefs, even in the face of danger and death. But never during those moments in Sabbath school and church had he thought *he'd* be called upon to demonstrate his faith so boldly.

Japan's attack on Hawaii's Pearl Harbor in December 1941 had thrown the United States into World War II. Draft notices informed a whole generation of young men of Uncle Sam's decision to make them part of their nation's fighting force. Doss reported immediately. Didn't the Bible teach that we should obey the laws of the land?

But there was a problem. Like Doss, many Christians refused to carry or fire a weapon of any kind. The same Bible that urged all to obey their government also commanded, in no uncertain terms, "Thou shalt not kill."

"I'll be happy to serve my country," Desmond told the military officer signing him in, "but I will not carry a gun. Let me put my energies into working as a medic, trained to treat wounded men on the battlefield."

So where did he end up? In a rifle company. Doss protested, and was eventually assigned to the medics, where he began training as a medical soldier.

He quickly learned how to use whatever material was at hand—saplings, rifle stocks—to form splints for broken arms and legs. He was taught how to administer blood plasma in the thick of battle, what to do for shock, when to provide water to the injured, and, just as important, when not to.

But hard work and dedication weren't enough to appease his tormentors.

"You guys are all alike," a sarcastic sergeant jeered one day.

"You talk big about religious freedom, but when your country needs you to help protect that freedom you chicken out."

"That's where you're wrong, Sergeant," Desmond responded respectfully. "I love this country just as much as you do. You won't find me failing to salute the flag or trying to get out of a work detail. I just refuse to kill, that's all."

There was another reason for Doss's unpopularity. He doggedly insisted on keeping the fourth commandment.

"Now what?" his superior groaned as the youthful noncombatant approached with a smart salute.

"Sir, I'd like to attend church services this Saturday as my beliefs dictate."

"Saturday!" The man chuckled. "You're a little confused, Private. The Army already allows its fighting force time off on Sunday."

"I understand, sir," the slender recruit pressed. "But I believe in the Bible Sabbath. That's the *seventh* day of the week, Saturday. God asks us to keep it holy by worshiping Him and refraining from all work. I'll be happy to do double duty on Sunday."

Reluctantly the man issued the Saturday pass to Desmond. In the battle of wills between the United States Army and Private Desmond T. Doss on the issue of Sabbath observance, someone would have to back down. And it wouldn't be Desmond.

Reveille pierced the hot morning air. "Rise and shine, you mama's boys," the sergeant roared as he paced down the length of the barracks. "Today we find out what you're really made of. And you'd better be ready. We've got 25 miles of full field-pack marching waiting for your enjoyment." The man paused at the door. "Oh yes, and you'll do it in eight hours."

"Hey, preacher!" a familiar voice called as the men assembled on the training ground. "No pass today?"

"He's got it made," another growled. "No rifle, no ammo—maybe he'll stop and pick some flowers along the way."

Doss grinned, but didn't bother to respond. His two canvas first-aid kits matched a rifle's weight and were twice as awkward. His Christian beliefs were cutting him no slack this day.

The march began. Soon sweat caused field uniforms to stick to their wearers like moist glue. As midday approached, the company staggered like zombies, eyes red, faces pale.

Suddenly a man fell. Desmond rushed to his side. His instructor's words echoed in his ear. "Clammy skin. Pulse barely readable. That's heat prostration."

Doss made the victim as comfortable as possible and turned him over to the ambulance that followed some distance behind. Then he had to run to catch up with his company.

High noon brought a lunch break. K-rations quickly disappeared down hungry throats. As Desmond took his first bite, another soldier slumped under a small tree and called for help. The man was examining a large blister on his heel.

"Do something," he pleaded.

"I'll try," Desmond reassured his comrade. He quickly pricked the blister with a sterile needle, doused the injured area with Merthiolate, then dressed it tightly with gauze. As he was finishing, another voice called out for help. Then another.

He continued attending hurting, aching men until the sergeant shouted, "Fall in. Now we go back!"

Injuries kept Desmond hopping for the entire return trip. He'd fix up a man as best he could, then rush to another. Despite his running around, he finished the march with the platoon. Even while lined up waiting for dismissal, three men passed out cold. Desmond hurried to their aid.

Soon all the soldiers were in their bunks with their shoes off. Doss still didn't rest. He checked every foot. That morning some had jeered him, calling him names. Now, lying exhausted, they watched the soft-spoken medic kneel by their bunks and treat their feet.

"Hey, preacher," one said, respect in his voice, "you're OK."

The jeering stopped, replaced by hesitant words of thanks and friendship.

For Desmond Doss and the other members of Company D, the future would hold another test. On a distant Pacific island unimagined horrors waited. On its rugged terrain

Desmond would be forced to search deep within himself and decide just how far he was willing to carry his belief and trust in the God he loved.

* * *

Desmond lay on his back, eyes closed. He could feel the dried blood pressing against his chest. His uniform reeked with sweat and grime, but he didn't care. He was too tired, too discouraged, too lonely to care.

The battle had been fierce. Images floated across his mind of torn and crumpled bodies, lifeless eyes staring at him from the depths of bomb craters, a bodiless hand still gripping a machine-gun stock.

Okinawa. Even the name of the island repulsed him.

"Hey, Doss," a voice whispered in the midnight stillness. "We're going to die tomorrow, aren't we?"

The young medic stirred. Without opening his eyes, he said, "Nah. We're going to make it OK. God'll take care of us."

"How come He didn't take care of those men this afternoon?" the voice asked. "They're dead. Stone dead. Where was God then?"

Desmond's fists clenched in the darkness. He didn't have an answer. He wished he did. He was wondering the same thing.

No! Doss sat up with a start. *I can't think that way.* His mind reeled. *God is here. He's always here!*

The medic's throat tightened as he battled with the voices in his head. *"I will never leave you nor forsake you." "I will never leave you nor forsake you."* He repeated the familiar Bible passage again and again. Finally exhaustion forced him into an uneasy sleep.

* * *

"Men"—Captain Vernon's voice carried across the battle-torn landscape—"the enemy has built a complex of pillboxes, fortifications, and emplacements. Two of our divisions have been cut to pieces trying to take that hill." He pointed north to a tall cliff guarding the narrow neck of land that led to the part of the island of Okinawa that remained to be taken. "Now it's up to us. We'll take our position at the bottom of the cliff. Then we'll climb up there and rip that piece of real estate right out of the hands of the Japanese. Let's go!"

The company quickly gathered at the base of the cliff and studied its rugged contours. One by one, men scaled the steep bank, then crept along on their bellies, collecting loose stones and pushing them together, trying to form a protective rock wall a few feet back from the edge of the cliff.

A rope was thrown down, allowing another squad of men to climb the vertical rampart.

Whump! Whump! Enemy knee mortars, capable of shooting almost straight up, sent volleys high into the air, followed by earth-shattering explosions as the shells slammed back into the soil. From this ground-based aerial attack there was no defense for the helpless members of Company D scurrying across the lip of the escarpment.

"Pull back!" the command rang out. "Retreat to the base!"

The next morning another attack was staged. With a newly installed rope cargo net now in place, the entire platoon could swarm the cliff as one body.

"This is going to be a dangerous mission, Doss," a superior admitted to his battle-weary medic. "You don't have to go."

Desmond nodded. "Sir, I may be needed. But I'd like to ask a favor before we start. You see, sir, I believe that prayer is the biggest lifesaver there is. I believe every man should have a word of prayer before he places his foot on the rope ladder to go up the escarpment."

By now all the soldiers who knew Desmond Doss realized that he was truly dedicated to his heavenly Father and believed his God could offer protection, even in the heat of battle.

The lieutenant turned and called out to his men. "Bow your heads," he commanded. "Doss is going to pray for us before we go."

Desmond was taken by surprise. He had meant that all should have a *personal* prayer. But not wanting to pass up an opportunity to speak to his Saviour on behalf of his friends, he bowed.

"Our Father," he prayed, "please give our lieutenant wisdom and understanding so he can give us the right orders, because our lives will be in his charge. Give each and every one of us wisdom, too, so we can be safe, if it be Thy will. Please, Lord, may we all come back alive. If there be any here who are not prepared to meet their Maker, let them prepare themselves now through prayer before they climb the cliff. We ask all this in Jesus' name."

The war on the escarpment stood still as the men remained motionless. Then confident, almost carefree, they turned to the cargo net and, along with Company A, started up the cliff.

The assault went well. Enemy emplacements were destroyed with satchel charges and flamethrowers. The forward squad raced along the summit, crushing dug-in Japanese soldiers with deadly precision.

When the fighting stopped, the Maeda escarpment was in American hands. But strangely, Company A had failed to take its assigned position. Their first five men to reach the top of the cliff had been killed instantly.

Through all the fighting, Desmond Doss's company had sustained only one minor injury—an officer was hit in the cheek by a piece of shrapnel. The men were amazed. Doss wasn't. Hadn't they prayed?

In the days that followed, fighting flared and subsided like a deadly tide. Then the fortunes of war turned. Out of secret holes in the ground and caves in the rocks, enemy soldiers poured forth, their chilling screams, the rat-tat-tat of automatic weapons, and the flat thud of exploding hand grenades filling the air.

The American soldiers suddenly found themselves on the run. At first the retreat was orderly, then the line broke as men ran for the cliff.

Soldiers scrambled down the cargo net, fighting their way back down the escarpment. Men hit by bullets and shells were left where they'd fallen, whether wounded or dead.

Doss, now the only remaining medic in the whole battalion, ran from fallen man to fallen man, doing what he could. He was too busy to realize the enemy was approaching. He didn't have time to think about the Japanese soldiers on the hilltop with him, shooting, throwing grenades, closing in with each second.

Friendly fire stopped the enemy advance literally dozens of feet from the lip of the cliff. Protected by the short stone wall his company had erected days before, Desmond Doss found himself alone on the hilltop, surrounded by dead and dying men. To the south, American forces were pummeling the Japanese. To the north, Japanese forces were straining to gain ground toward the cliff's summit.

The gentle, soft-spoken medic with the wavy brown hair was caught in the crossfire with nowhere to go but over the cliff.

But what about the wounded? He couldn't just leave them there. They'd surely die at the hands of the approaching enemy.

"God," the soldier with no gun cried out above the din of battle, "help me! Please help me!"

The answer to his prayer came not as a gun-silencing miracle from heaven, but as a voice speaking quietly to his heart. Above the roar of battle he heard his heavenly Father whisper, "The men, Desmond. Save the men around you."

He responded immediately. Grabbing a wounded soldier nearby, Doss pulled him to the precipice. Securing a rope around the man's waist and chest, he tested the knots. Satisfied, he simply pushed the moaning combatant over the edge.

"Take him off!" Doss shouted down at the men trying to steady the swaying form hanging at the end of the rope far below. "I've got more wounded up here. Get him to the aid station *fast!* He's dying."

The injured soldier cried out in pain as hands loosened the knots and lowered him gently into a waiting stretcher. He caught a quick glimpse of the end of the rope speeding back up the cliff.

Doss squirmed on his belly behind the protective rock wall. Enemy bullets sparked and chipped away at the stones inches above his head. But the medic didn't stop or even pause in his desperate attempt to reach the other conscious and unconscious wounded lying all along the crest of the war-ravaged escarpment.

He slipped another man's legs through loops in his rope and pulled him to the edge. Quickly he passed the tether around the soldier's chest and tied a secure knot.

The men at the base of the cliff saw another form slip from the summit and drop along its rough earthen face, loosening dirt and pebbles as it slid in their direction. Desmond strained, his heels digging into the stony soil, trying to keep the bound man from picking up too much speed. The medic's fingers burned as the rope slid through his palms.

"Get him back to the aid station nonstop!" Doss shouted above the rattle of machine guns and *thump-thump* of mortars. Heavy dust thrown up by exploding shells drifted along the cliff, making his work even more dangerous.

As quickly as he could, Desmond lowered one man after another to the base of the escarpment. Several times he had to lift his head above the protective wall in order to fasten his rope around a wounded man. Why no Japanese bullet slammed through his helmet he didn't know. *God must be with me today* was all he could think.

Doss remained on top of the cliff until he'd lowered every wounded man to safety. The unofficial count placed the total lives saved at 100 men. "Couldn't have been more than 50," Desmond humbly insisted later. For the official war record, the number was a compromising 75.

Only after all the wounded had reached the bottom of the escarpment did the soft-spoken medic who refused to carry a gun scramble down the cargo net. Desmond had single-handedly saved the lives of more than half the men who'd taken part in the assault.

* * *

The war in the Pacific ground on, taking a terrible toll in lives, both American and Japanese. During one battle

Desmond Doss was seriously wounded while trying to save a comrade's life. For the gentle noncombatant the war was finally over.

Sent home to his family, friends, and wife, Doss was welcomed by a thankful nation. When he was well enough to travel, he received an invitation he'd never forget.

"The president? of the United States?" The young man's mouth dropped opened.

"That's right," a visitor named Colonel Conner said with a nod. "I'm to inform you that you've been awarded the Congressional Medal of Honor, our country's highest honor."

So it was that on October 12, 1945, on the White House lawn in Washington, D.C., President Truman stood before Desmond Doss, extending a grateful hand. With a smile the president turned to the assembled crowd and proudly listened as a citation outlining the Seventh-day Adventist medic's heroism was read for all to appreciate.

But the story doesn't end there. There were many more battles waiting for Desmond Doss. Not on some fire-swept enemy island in the Pacific. Not on a cliff top where the scream of ricocheting bullets ripped the air.

The new battles came silently. Doss contracted tuberculosis several years later, underwent dozens of painful surgeries and treatments for his war wounds, and faced financial ruin when a business he started with his life savings was accidentally destroyed.

Desmond Doss faced each battle with the same God-fearing determination he'd shown under fire. During those years of personal and financial war, he helped in the creation of a Seventh-day Adventist military medical training camp in Michigan. Here Christian young men and women learned how to save lives in war instead of destroying them. Church officials insisted on naming the facility "Camp Desmond Doss."

Thousands of children and older folk thrilled at the stories Desmond told while traveling from camp meeting to camp meeting across the nation. He always gave the glory to God.

And today, if you were to attend the little Seventh-day

Adventist church in Rising Fawn, Georgia, you'd sit in a simple sanctuary built, log by log, by the man who saved 75 lives that day on the escarpment.

Heaven will be filled with heroes. And Desmond Doss will lead the songs of praise to the One who, long ago, showed the world how to place others first and self last.

HIDDEN DANGER

by Helen Heavirland

VR-R-ROOO-OO-OOOM. *Vr-r-roo-oo-oom*. The roar of the other motorcycles faded into the distance ahead.

I'd better get moving, 14-year-old Mike thought. *Jim and Uncle Glen know these logging roads. I don't.*

He tugged his helmet strap a little tighter, then kicked the starter. His metal-flake green Yamaha Enduro roared, and he took off in a cloud of dust.

Mike liked the smell of mountain pine and dust and motorcycle exhaust all mixed up together. He loved the thrill of power under his control.

The engine roared and purred, roared and purred as he shifted. *I've gotta catch up with them*, he told himself. He shifted into fifth and opened the throttle wide.

The wind slapped at Mike's goggles and face, making the 90 degree air feel cooler. He seemed to fly over the bumps and ruts, around corners, up hills and down.

Mike concentrated so intently on catching up with his cousin and uncle that he didn't notice the adjoining trails he passed. Had he missed the one he should have turned onto?

This doesn't look familiar, he suddenly noticed. The thought jolted him for a second. *Of course it doesn't*, he tried to convince himself. *I can't possibly know every tree in the Cascades*. But the facts that he didn't know the road very well and that Jim and Uncle Glen were a long way ahead didn't comfort him any.

The road seemed narrower than Mike remembered from the trip into the mountains several hours before. But he and his cycle flew on.

"Stop! You missed the turnoff!" Mike barely heard the shout over the engine roar. But he understood the words distinctly.

How could I have gotten ahead of Jim and Uncle Glen? Mike wondered. He eased the throttle and glanced behind. No bikes. No one was there. He looked again. *Weird,* he thought. *I'm not used to hearing voices!*

Mike gunned the engine again. *I have to catch up!* He leaned into another corner.

"Stop!" the same voice screamed. "You missed the turnoff!"

Mike clenched the hand brake and jammed his right foot on the brake pedal. Dust billowed up as the cycle slid to a stop. He peered through the settling dust. The blood drained from his face. His whole body began to tremble.

Ten feet ahead of his cycle a cliff dropped at least 100 feet. There were no warning signs. No guardrails. The mountain trail just stopped at the top of the precipice.

For an instant Mike visualized himself and his bike hurtling down . . . down . . . down . . . He knew he wouldn't have walked away.

Switching the engine off, Mike kicked down the stand. He crawled off his cycle. Still trembling, he leaned against a sturdy-looking pine.

After several minutes Mike realized the intensity of the silence. All he heard was an occasional bird song. And a grasshopper that flew up from the grass. He couldn't hear the other motorcycles. Not even in the distance. He looked around. No bikes. Nobody. He looked at the road. His own slide to a stop was recorded in the dust. There were no other tracks.

Who hollered for Mike to stop? Mike thinks he'll recognize the voice when he meets his guardian angel one day.

THE NIGHT THE DACOITS CAME

by Isabelle Sargunam

TAT-TAT-TAT-TAT! Tat-tat-tat-tat!

The staccato sound shattered the quiet of the evening.

Startled, Bella looked up from the book she was reading.

"Why, that sounds like machine-gun firing," she said to herself. "And it seems to be in the street behind our house."

She was living in postwar Burma, where the law and order situation was far from normal. There was adequate police protection in the capital city, but it was almost nil in the suburbs and districts. So armed gangs of men called dacoits looted the countryside and even made attacks on boats and trains.

Bella's father was the Indian doctor in charge of a small government hospital at Insein, a suburb seven miles from Rangoon, the capital of Burma. Another physician lived on the street behind her house.

"So they weren't just rumors after all," she mused aloud. "It's really happening!" There had been a lot of talk about the dacoits making doctors' homes their special targets.

Day was fading and it would soon be dark. Bella hated the dark. To her overwrought imagination, it was peopled with evil men who crept stealthily into homes with machine guns and other modern weapons to wreak destruction.

What was she to do? She was all alone in the house. Her father hadn't returned from the hospital. Her mother was visiting a married daughter in Rangoon, and the other sister had gone to shop in the city.

According to the style of the old wooden houses in Burma, an entire side, usually the front portion, was made up of doors. They could be folded back to let in the cool air when the days were hot and muggy and the nights still and stifling.

Bella knew that she should close the four big doors that opened onto the veranda, but she was too frightened to move. She sat listening to the screams and yells that seemed to come from right in back of her house.

"Bella, why didn't you close the doors?"

The girl jumped up when she heard the voice. She had not been aware of anyone's coming up the stairs.

It was Frank, the tall, thin, reserved young man who lived on the opposite side of the street. He had hardly exchanged half a dozen words with Bella whenever they met, but now she was happy and thankful for his company.

"Oh, I'm so glad you came," she said.

He quickly pulled the doors shut and bolted them. Then easing himself into a chair, he said, "The dacoits are attacking the lady doctor's house, which is on the main road one street away from ours."

"How do you know?" she asked.

"The medical student who lives next door to you watched from a distance and came back and told us. Mamma sent me here to stay with you since you are alone."

Suddenly there was the sound of running feet and voices. Bella lifted her frightened eyes toward the young man seated opposite her.

"It's all right," he said. "They are only people from our street who went to watch."

"I'm glad of that."

"I wonder which gang attacked this evening," he mused. She looked up at him, puzzled. He saw the look and smiled. "You see, there are many gangs of dacoits, but the terror-striking group are known as the 'Black Shirts' because they always wear black shirts or vests and black shorts and appear without warning at different suburbs in big lorries or trucks."

Bella shivered. "I hope they will never come to our street!"

As she was speaking, her father came to the door and was let in by Frank. He was so happy to see Bella safe and sound. He had heard that the dacoits were looting the other doctor's home and he thanked Frank over and over for staying with Bella.

The one absorbing topic at supper that evening was the surprise attack of the dacoits. Bella and her mother were Adventists, and during worship they asked the Lord to protect them and keep them under the shadow of His wings.

"Do you think they will come here, Father?" asked Bella.

"I don't know," he answered and Bella was glad to hear him add, "We can only trust God to keep us safe."

Two uneventful days passed. Bella tried to keep her thoughts away from dacoits and guns.

On the third night, a full moon turned the sleepy little suburb into a fairyland of silver. Children played hopscotch and catch on the street. A young man strummed a guitar on the opposite porch, and the strains of a peaceful Burmese song from the radio next door came to Bella's ears.

"It's so good to be alive!" she said to herself.

Before going to bed that night, she prayed earnestly for God's protection over them while they slept.

Her last thoughts before drifting off to sleep were of the great changes that had come to the land of her birth—beautiful Burma, with its happy, laughing people.

She suddenly awoke. Was it a dream? What was that sound? A truck was driving into her street. It stopped just a few doors away.

What did it mean?

Bella's heart was hammering against her ribs. Her mouth

and throat were dry. She felt weak and cold. Then she felt a touch on her arm and her mother's voice whispered, "Pray."

Bella's bed was in the front room. She strained her ears to catch some sound, but there was only silence for two or three minutes. Then the truck door banged. There was the heavy, measured tread of booted feet. They stopped in front of her house. She could clearly hear whispering. Then footsteps on the stairs! Silence for a few seconds, followed by loud knocking.

"We want to see the doctor," a voice called out in Burmese.

"Why do you want to see him?" her father asked.

Bella saw her father with a spear in his hand, and her brother-in-law, who was an army officer, holding a revolver and standing a few paces away from the door. Her mother stood in front of them, begging them with her actions not to fire. She kept pointing up with her hand. She was asking them to trust God.

"We have an urgent case at home," came the voice from outside the house.

"There are four other doctors in this area. Why don't you call one of them?"

"No, we want you."

Bella's father stood looking at the floor for a few seconds. Then he raised his head and said, "I'm sorry. I don't go out after 10:00 p.m."

The furious drumming of her heart continued. What would happen next? Would they use guns to break the door open? She knew that they must be dacoits, trying cunning to enter their home.

The footsteps descended. There was whispering again, then the sounds of boots reascending the short flight of steps.

"O God!" pleaded Bella desperately. "Keep these wicked men from killing us."

"Doctor, you must come with us. The patient is about to deliver a baby, but there are complications. We must have an experienced doctor like you for this case."

"If this is a delivery, it will be better for you to call the doctor on the main road behind my house. She is more experienced in handling such cases."

"But we want you to come," the voice insisted.

"I'm sorry. I cannot come."

The boots descended. There was a whispered consultation and then the sound of returning footsteps.

"We are desperate. The woman is dying. Why can't you come with us?"

"Your case is not so desperate. You have four other doctors to choose from. I cannot come. I'm sorry, but I don't go out after 10:00 p.m."

There was a moment's silence. Then the repetition of boots descending . . . whispering.

"O Lord, keep them from shooting," agonized Bella. "We are so weak and defenseless. We are in Your hands."

The short time that it took to enact this drama seemed an eternity to Bella.

"Please, Lord, send them away. We trust in You," she prayed.

Then came the welcome sounds of heavy boots walking back on the tarred road, followed by the banging of metal doors. The engine came to life and the truck roared away in the night.

Her mother's voice broke the ensuing silence.

"Let us thank God for saving us from these terrible men. I have no doubt that they were dacoits."

Weak and sweating, Bella got out of bed to kneel with the others. It was almost 1:00 a.m., and there was no more sleep for the doctor's household that night.

Early the next morning, their neighbors told them of the drama they had witnessed from behind closed doors and curtained windows.

A truckload of Black Shirts had driven into the street. They had a consultation beside the truck, and then ten armed men had walked up to her home. They told of the whispered consultations and of the lone dacoit who had acted as the go-between and the speaker.

Commenting on their sudden decision to leave, the neighbors said, "We can't understand why they left in such an abrupt manner. We have never heard of such a happening before."

"We prayed to our great God and He made them go away," Bella's mother explained.

The Buddhist neighbors nodded solemnly and walked away.

As Bella went up the steps, she softly repeated to herself Psalm 37:40: "He shall deliver them from the wicked, and save them, because they trust in him."

SWAMP FEARS

by Richard Maffeo

RICKY BREATHED IN deeply as the cool air rushed past his face. He enjoyed this time of year. Almost more than summer. Especially now that the humid days of August were over. He stared out the open car window as they raced past pastureland where cattle grazed lazily. Old wooden fence posts hung themselves from sagging barbed wire. Every once in a while a forgotten bale of hay could be seen rotting in the middle of a field. He knew from the change in landscape they were almost there.

When his friend Steve and his family moved away from the apartment complex where they had been neighbors, they both vowed to remain pen pals. Maybe even call each other once in a while, if their parents wouldn't object. And Ricky was glad his dad had driven him to Steve's eleventh birthday party in July. It was a great party.

"We're here," Dad broke into his thoughts.

Ricky leaned forward to see out the windshield. Steve was standing on the black asphalt driveway, waving his hands at them.

Steve and his family were among the first homeowners in the new housing subdivision on Long Island. Whenever Ricky's family visited Steve's, the boys spent hours—whole days—running across acres of open farmland and marsh in various stages of conversion to houses, parks, schools, and shopping areas.

Almost as soon as the car stopped, Ricky and Steve set about planning their afternoon exploring adventure. In short order, they found themselves perched atop the rafters of a partially constructed home at the far side of the vast construction site.

"Hey, let's climb into that one over there," Steve suggested. "Beat ya to it!" he shouted, dropping to the floor and racing toward it.

And so the day wore on. Neither Steve nor Ricky noticed the sun sinking lower in the sky.

"What's over there?" Ricky pointed toward a field of cattails.

"Nothin' special," Steve answered. Then he challenged, "Let's play hide and seek. Hide your eyes and count to a hundred." Without waiting for a reply, he raced off into the weeds.

"Ready or not, here I come!" Ricky yelled. The cattails swayed gracefully as he forced his way through them, pushing farther and farther toward the middle of the field. They were tall cattails—taller than he was. And they were so thick he could push through them only with great effort.

But they were not his only concern. The darkening sky had finally caught his attention. He stopped plowing through the weeds and scanned in all directions. He couldn't see a thing except the thin pale stalks around him and the rapidly darkening sky above.

"Hey, Steve!" Ricky's stomach churned.

No answer.

"Steven!" he called a little louder. His ears strained against the ever-rustling grasses. His mouth felt parched.

"Steven! Where are you? I'm not playing anymore." He listened. "Steven!"

Silence. Except for the cattails.

Then he heard it . . . or did he? Yes! There it was again. He could hear his name above the soft rustling of the wind in the cattails. But from which direction? "Riiiiickyyyy!" a voice called. "Riiiiickyyyy!"

"Here! Over here," Ricky shouted back. Breathing faster, he pushed into the wall of weeds. "Steeeeevennnnn!

Where are you?"

"Over here!" Steve sounded closer.

At last Ricky heard him crunch-crunching nearby. In a moment they faced each other. Sweat beaded on their flushed faces.

"Where were you?" Ricky accused. "It got dark pretty quick, and I figured we'd better be gettin' home."

"I was looking for you," Steve defended himself.

"Well, come on," Ricky urged, not wanting to waste any more time. "Let's get outta here."

"Which way is out?"

Ricky looked at him, his face blank. "Don't you know?"

Steve shook his head.

"But . . . but you live here!" Ricky said in disbelief.

"Yeah, but I've never been here before. At least not in the dark."

"Well," Ricky said finally. "Let's go this way." He pointed to the left.

Without speaking, they lunged against the weeds. The only sound breaking the silence was the dry grass crunching beneath their feet.

After a long time Ricky said, "I think we're lost." Steve didn't answer.

"What are we gonna do?" Ricky stopped. Fear gnawed at his stomach.

Steve looked like he'd been crying. "I don't know." He shrugged his shoulders hopelessly. "Maybe if we called out for help?"

"Helllllllp!" they chorused together.

They stood quietly, listening . . .

Nothing.

They tried again. And again. And again. But only the soft rustle of the cattails broke the stillness.

"Maybe we should pray," Steve said.

Wiping the sweat from his face, Ricky nodded. In the years their families had known each other, neither boy could remember ever hearing God mentioned, except as a swear word or a casual exclamation of surprise. But now, lost in a tangle of fear and desperation, they both knew this situation called for help far beyond their capabilities.

They closed their eyes and prayed in earnest for God to help them find their way home. Then they started walking. After a time, the ground began to feel soggy beneath their muddied shoes. Before long they broke through to a clearing. The glassy calm waters of the bay lapped the shore at their feet. And across the water was home.

"Doesn't look very far away," Steve estimated.

Ricky shook his head. "No, it doesn't. Do you think we could swim it?"

They stared at the water. Finally, Ricky sighed in resignation. "Maybe not."

Steve agreed. And once again the boys turned back to the weeds, both sobbing openly as they trudged on. Every now and then they prayed aloud, "God, please help us."

Then suddenly, it happened. Just like that. They broke through to another clearing. Wood-framed houses rose before them—the same ones they'd been playing in earlier that day.

"We made it!" Steve shouted, his eyes dancing. "Oh, thank You, God! We made it!"

In the many years that followed, Ricky and Steve lost track of each other. But Ricky can certainly remember back to that day when, lost in the cattails, certain disaster was averted as two boys turned their backs to the bay and pushed on into the darkness. And he still thanks God for bringing them safely home.

I should know, because I'm Ricky.

DELIVERANCE

by Stephen Fleming

NOW HEAR THIS," the voice on the intercom speaker crackled into our ears. "All hands lay up to the gun deck at thirteen hundred (one o'clock). The captain will speak to you there."

I was the electrician striker on the *Hammering Hank,* a nickname given by the Marines at Iwo Jima to our destroyer mine layer. Yes, the *Henry A. Wiley,* D.M. 29, as she was properly called, had made quite a name for herself. She was a fearless fighting ship who could hold her bow high. We were now in Okinawa. The invasion of that island, in which we had played an important part, had been successful.

"Wonder what's up?" remarked Randy, one of our best buddies. "Maybe we're going home."

"Huh! Big chance we've got of that," answered Bob Seely. "We'll probably make a raid on Japan next. I hear they're going to invade—"

"Nah, we'll probably hit China next," I interrupted. "Well, it's almost thirteen hundred now. Let's get up there and see."

We hustled up to the gun deck, pausing now and then to ask others if they knew what the captain was going to say. Everybody had a theory, but no one knew.

At exactly thirteen hundred Commander Bjaranson marched onto the gun deck.

"Men," he opened his speech, "I've called you all here to tell you about our next operation. We have been assigned to radar picket duty. That is, we will steam around a certain position about 100 miles from the island. Our job will be to spot enemy aircraft with our radar device. Then we will radio their position to the airfield. The Air Force will in turn send planes out to intercept them before they can raid the island. We will get underway at fourteen-thirty. That's all. Dismissed."

Our picket station, number 12, which lay directly between Okinawa and Japan, was only one of a network that completely encircled the island. The Japanese rightfully blamed us for the fact that they could not reach American positions with their bombs, and evidently decided that they must first get rid of the radar patrols. Approximately four times each day the planes swarmed over us, attempting to erase us from the surface of the water. They attacked us in every conceivable way: bombs, torpedoes, machine guns, and finally suicide planes. The suicide attacks were the most deadly. In this method of warfare the pilot would try to crash his plane, loaded with explosives, into a ship. Many ships were sunk by this method of attack. Somehow my ship was never hit.

On a certain July Fourth, at about 11:30 in the morning, my buddies and I were sitting on our lockers singing such songs as "Down by the Old Mill Stream" and "When Irish Eyes Are Smiling," when suddenly the general alarm started its bing, bing, bing, bing, bing, and a voice boomed, "All hands to general quarters."

Immediately the whole ship was in commotion. Men, like ants, scurried about the decks of the trim ship. In a few seconds we had all reached our battle stations. Then I realized that there were no enemy planes in sight. There was only a blue, almost cloudless sky covering the gently swelling expanse of royal blue water.

I wondered why we had been alerted, but I was not kept wondering long. Suddenly the loudspeaker boomed, "This is your captain speaking. We have just received word that the three ships on radar picket station 13 have just been sunk. We are the nearest ship to that area, so we will attempt to rescue the survivors."

The radio message had stated that picket station number 13 had undergone a tremendous air attack, which had consisted of *Kamikaze* (suicide) planes and also Baka bombs.

"What are Baka bombs?" I asked my gunnery officer.

"Oh, they're rocket planes that carry about a ton of TNT in their noses. It's another suicide weapon, only these planes dive at better than 800 miles per hour."

"Eight hundred miles per hour! Wow!" exclaimed Kovack, gunner.

"Let's hope we don't see any," I moaned.

Tensely we waited as our prow turned toward the position where our sister ships had met with disaster. Eyes strained, ears alert, men stood silent as our destroyer plowed toward her destination. Looking back, we could see our escort of little gunboats, staying behind.

Then we were nearing the area that had been claimed by destruction. All seemed peaceful and calm. A beautiful rainbow had formed in the fine salt spray that was thrown up by our bow.

Suddenly they were upon us! Planes careened at us from all directions.

"Action starboard!" screamed the loudspeaker. "Plane coming in off the starboard bow." "Mount two action port, plane high off the port beam." "Mount three, get that Betty coming in on the port quarter."

"Voom, voom, voom!" came the five-inch guns.

"Bam, bam-bam, bam-bam, bam," thundered the forties.

"Wang, wang, wang, wang," sang the twenties.

The rapid staccato of the 50-caliber machine guns presided over all the rest of the din.

"That's one of ours! It's a Corsair," shouted someone.

"Here comes a Grace off the port quarter. Get her!" barked another voice.

Clink, crack, crack, clink.

"What's that?"

"Shrapnel! Duck!"

"That's a Baka bomb. Get it!"

"There goes its wing."

"That was close!"

By this time the ship was covered with heavy gun smoke that smelled like sulfur matches, and the deck was littered with a profusion of empty powder cases and other debris.

"Action port. Plane low; get him," came the voice from the speaker.

Peering around trying to penetrate the smoke, I could see that an airplane was attacking from the port bow. From the distance it looked like a gull wavering, then zig-zagging back and forth. Now it was climbing. Now it was dropping. But always it came closer.

"Plenty of time to get this baby," I thought. "What's wrong with him anyway? Plenty of time. No need to get excited. But why haven't they got him yet? They will. I hope they will. But what if they don't? If he keeps coming on the same course that he's on now, he'll hit right here! Why can't they stop him?"

When it looked as if we were doomed to death, suddenly I remembered my mother's telling me that even though we may be unworthy, God still hears our prayers, and that if He sees fit, He will protect us. A few phrases of Psalm 23 popped into my mind: "Yea, though I walk through the valley of the shadow—" With my eyes still fixed on the plane that was speedily approaching, I breathed a prayer: "O Lord, I know that I'm not worthy. I know I'm a terrible sinner, but, please, please, God, save me. Help me! If it's all right with You—if it's Your will—please send an angel here to protect me—quick, Lord!"

The plane continued to come closer and closer. It was obvious that nothing we could do would stop its grim approach. Again I shouted in supplication: "O Lord, save me!"

Then something marvelous happened. Suddenly, for no apparent reason, the plane went into a steep climb, rolled over, and passed overhead. Looking up, I could see the face of the pilot. The tip of our mast was touched by the tip of his wing; it vibrated violently. The aircraft spun around, went out of sight for a moment, then returned and crashed into the water on the opposite side of the ship from where I was standing.

In a moment the lookout bawled, "Men in the water—off the starboard bow."

The destroyer turned and cruised over to the shuddering men huddled around life rafts and boards and debris that would keep them afloat. Many of these men were injured, some by the explosives of their ships, some by the machine-gun fire of the planes that had strafed them while they were struggling in the water. Gently we lifted them from the water and gave them first aid. Then they were sent to hospital ships that were awaiting them. I shall long remember the mangled arms and limbs of those men who had been bitten by hunger-mad sharks.

As we steamed back to our own picket station, the men of our crew discussed the strange actions of the airplane, which, in line with all the science of flying, should have struck us.

"I think that the gunner was hit by a small bullet, and re-acting to the pain, drew back on the stick," asserted one of our men.

"My best guess is that a bullet must've got stuck in the el-evators," theorized another.

Noticing my silence, Randy turned to me: "What do you think, Steve?"

"I prayed," I whispered briefly.

"Me too," he murmured.

Randy and I were sure that we had the true explanation. Whenever I hear someone say that there is no God or that there is no power or validity in prayer, I tell him of the events of July 4, 1945.

PARABLES 'N' STUFF

5

THE TRIAL OF SHARON OF SHARON

by Celeste perrino Walker

AND IT CAME to pass that in the tenth year of Principal Thomas O'Dooley's reign in the junior high school of Meadowcrest, a certain girl called Sharon of Sharon was brought unto him that she might be punished. Thus she was dragged to the office of Principal O'Dooley by the teacher Miss Needlemeyer, with much wailing and gnashing of teeth.

Principal O'Dooley arose from the desk whence he judgeth good and evil in the school called Meadowcrest to make this proclamation: "O Needlemeyer, why hast thou brought to me such a belligerent and unyielding child? Thinkest thou that she may yet repent of the crimes she hast committed?"

"Verily, verily I say unto thee," began Miss Needlemeyer, "I bring to thee Sharon of Sharon, who hast not heeded the words of her teacher, namely myself. She continueth to break the rules of the class called English. I demand that she be punished according to the fullest extent of the law." Thus spake her teacher unto Principal O'Dooley.

"Sharon of Sharon, what hast thou to say for thyself? Breaketh thou the rules of thy teacher, Needlemeyer?"

And Sharon of Sharon raised up her hair-sprayed head and looked deep into the eyes of Principal O'Dooley. "O sir, I beg of thee, do not cast me away from thy presence before I have had a chance to explain to thee the course of my misdeeds and defend before thee my actions. Show compassion unto thy servant—er, student."

Principal O'Dooley's eyes narrowed as he regarded the words spoken by Sharon of Sharon. "I say to thee this day that thou mightest have a moment to come forth and defend thine actions before I expel thee. O Needlemeyer, what say thee of this misconduct? How acted thy student called Sharon of Sharon?"

"Truly I say unto thee, during the class called English, Sharon of Sharon approached the storehouse of books, called closet, and removed a tome [that's a book] from the innermost recesses. That book is now missing. Sharon of Sharon also faileth to raise her hand before she speaketh, and cheweth the wad called gum during class. And she doth not pass in the papers called homework. These are but a few of the misdeeds of the student called Sharon of Sharon." Then sitteth Miss Needlemeyer down to await further proclamation from Principal O'Dooley.

"Arise, Sharon of Sharon, and defend thy actions before me," spake Principal O'Dooley in a loud and commanding voice.

Then arose Sharon of Sharon and wept as she made her case before Principal O'Dooley. "O sir, it is true that I chew the wad called gum and neglect to pass in the papers called homework, but of the book, I knoweth not anything. It was a fellow classmate who removed it from the storehouse called closet."

"Then say thee that these accusations brought against thee by Needlemeyer are true?" bellowed Principal O'Dooley as he shuffled the scrolls and parchments upon his desk.

"Yes, but, sir," cried Sharon of Sharon, "the rules of Needlemeyer are many, and it is impossible to fulfill them all!"

At which time entereth Mr. Hermon of the class called science. "Halt! Halt ye the trial of Sharon of Sharon!" he called forth as he confronted Principal O'Dooley and Miss Needlemeyer. "I am here to plead on behalf of my pupil, one Sharon of Sharon, the brightest of stars ever to take my class called science. Dost thou think it possible that she breaketh a rule? Nay! Thinkest thou that she is capable of disobeying an order? Nay! I say unto thee, repent from thine accusations while there is yet time!"

Principal O'Dooley stood as one smitten, his mouth hanging open like the great Sheep Gate. "What knoweth thee of the accusations brought before me in the innermost recesses of my office called principal?" demanded Principal O'Dooley. "Sharon of Sharon hath already admitted her guilt and convinceth me that she is worthy of my most awful punishment."

Mr. Hermon collapseth into a chair with a moan. "Nay! It is impossible. Sharon of Sharon is a sweet and gentle child, who never breaketh a rule, speaketh out of turn, or pulleth a fast one, for she loveth the class called science."

"Mr. Hermon speaketh the truth," noted Sharon of Sharon. "Indeed, I loveth the class called science and wouldst never think to harm in any way my teacher, Mr. Hermon."

"And just what maketh the difference between the class called science and the class called English?" demanded Miss Needlemeyer with haughty scorn upon her brow.

"The path in the class called English is hard, the rules art tedious, and swift is the punishment for those who disobey. I keep them out of fear until I grow weary," explained Sharon of Sharon. "The class called science is full of joy and happiness. I love to keep the rules of the teacher called Hermon. They art not burdensome to me."

At the words of Sharon of Sharon, Miss Needlemeyer was smitten in her heart, and she repented and rent her garments, clothing herself with sackcloth, and adorning her head with ashes. "Forgive me, O Sharon of Sharon. I knew not my commands to be burdensome. What must I do that the class called English may be joyful and happy?"

"O Miss Needlemeyer," cried Sharon of Sharon, "it would be easy to love the class called English and to keep its rules if they were made in the spirit of love. Then wouldst I rise up and call thee blessed, and thy rules would be a joy to keep. For it is from a heart filled with love whence springeth forth obedience."

Then Miss Needlemeyer embraceth Sharon of Sharon. "From this day forward, the rules of the class called English will be made out of love for its students. And I, thy teacher Needlemeyer, wilt love thee as well."

Then sayeth Principal O'Dooley, "Thus concludeth the trial of Sharon of Sharon. Miss Needlemeyer will henceforth issue her rules in love, which all her students will obey with great happiness."

Then entered Principal O'Dooley the trial of Sharon of Sharon into the parchment roll called record book, to be seen by generations to come. For in time it might come to pass that rules would become harsh again and break the spirits of the students of the junior high school called Meadowcrest.

And there was joy among the people gathered in the office called principal (and among those outside who listened in), and they rejoiced with much wiping of the eyes and blowing of the nose. And they departed each one to his own way in peace and good will.

SCRIPTURE SHOOTOUT

by Randy Fishell

WADE BOOKMAN TOOK a sip of Garbanzo Cooler, then set down his glass. His gaze swept around the table, a sinister smile crossing his face as he slapped down each card of a winning hand.

"Matthew, Mark, Luke . . ." the man paused for effect, then flung out the final card, ". . . and John." Groans came from around the table as the others threw in their cards.

"Bookman, I'll get you at 'Scripture Fours' yet!" Parley Brown, a cowhand from the nearby Circle V, complained. "I already had me a Love, a Joy, and a Peace. If'n I'd a-had me a Kindness, you'da been finished!"

"Yeah, sure, Parley," Bookman responded coolly. "Maybe next time."

As Bookman's defeated opponents stood to leave, Parley noticed a tall figure stroll by the window. Seconds later, the doorway of the Short Branch Cafe darkened, and the room grew silent.

Wade Bookman's moustache twitched slightly.

The saloon-style cafe doors swung slowly open, and in stepped . . . Turner Page.

Page's cold, hard eyes narrowed as he scanned the room.

The stranger swaggered over to where Wade Bookman sat shuffling his deck of cards.

"You Bookman?" he sneered.

"That's the *last* half of what most people call me. The first half is . . . '*Mister*.'"

"I hear you've got a reputation, Bookman," Page continued, bearing down.

"That depends."

"They say you're the best in these parts. Is that what *you* say?" Page leaned over the table and drew within inches of Bookman's face.

"This is gonna get ugly," Parley whispered to "Slim" Johnson.

Bookman set down his cards, then stared at Page. "I don't believe I caught *your* name, Mister . . ."

"Does the name Turner Page ring a bell?" the stranger growled.

Bookman paused. "It's passed through town a time or two."

"Well, maybe it's time it hung around a while. Whatd'ya say, Bookman? You wanna tangle with 'Mister' Page, or are you scared of losin' your 'reputation'?"

Bookman snorted. "Page, I can beat you with one hand tied to a hitching post."

"In that case, you won't mind steppin' outside and puttin' your brains where your mouth is."

"Huh?"

"I'm callin' you out, Bookman!" Page's gravelly voice roared. "This town ain't big enough for two Scripture slingers."

"Parley, you'd better sneak on outta here and get word to the marshal about what's goin' down," Slim Johnson urged. "This here gospel gunfight could get outta hand real quick."

"I reckon you're right." The cowhand silently inched his way over toward the door, then slipped outside unnoticed.

* * *

"Are you sure it's Page, Parley?" Marshal Wilton swung his legs off the desk and stood up.

"If I'm-a lyin' I'm-a dyin', Marshal. He's got a OT-NT 66 Special strapped to his leg with his name engraved on it in gold letters."

The marshal let out a soft whistle. "Bookman's not used to that kind of firepower." He turned to his deputy. "Fessup, we'd better get over there and put a stop to this before somebody gets hurt. Two men like Bookman and Page takin' aim at each other could tear this town to pieces."

"I'm right behind ya, Marshal."

"As usual."

* * *

A hot wind swirled the dust on Main Street. Inside, folks peered out cautiously from behind curtains; pairs of children's eyeballs bobbed up and down at windowsill level, each hoping to catch a glimpse of the activity out on the street.

"You ready, Bookman?" Turner Page shouted from 20 paces away.

"I'm *always* ready." His moustache twitched slightly.

Silence. A dog barked in the distance. Seconds passed. Then, with a lightning-quick motion, Turner Page drew his Bible from its holster. The glint of the noontime sun on its gold-leaf edges took Bookman by surprise. Half-blinded, he dived to the ground, rolled to the side of the street, then leaped behind the rain barrel perched in front of Grisby's General Store. Stunned by his archrival's sudden movements, Page ran for the cover of a horse watering trough on the opposite side of Main Street.

"You're spineless, Bookman!" Page called out, breathing hard. "But if this is how you're gonna play out your hand, have it your way. Let's see how you handle this, hotshot! Where in the Bible do you find instructions for clearing a railroad pass through the Rockies?"

Within earshot of the activity, Marshal Wilton raised a hand, stopping Fessup and Parley in their tracks. "Hold up right here." The three men pressed against a wall. "Listen."

Behind the rain barrel, Wade Bookman shook his head and

laughed. "Page, Page. Is that the best you can do?" He pulled a tiny New Testament from his vest pocket. "But for your sake—and the railroad's . . ." *BANG!* "Matthew 17:20 and 21: 'If you have faith as small as a mustard seed, you can say to this mountain, "Move from here to there" and it will move.'"

"But, Marshal," Fessup whispered, "that passage don't have anything to do with the railroad!"

"Quiet, Fessup. There's more talkin'."

"You got lucky, Bookman," Page snapped.

"Luck didn't buy me this reputation. But maybe this'll cost you yours! Tell me from Scripture where Eustace Billings hid his gold strike before he left for his nephew's weddin' last week!"

"What!" Fessup gasped. "How can the Bible—"

"Come, come, now, 'Mister' Bookman," Page chuckled. "Even a half-brain would know precisely where to find the gold if he knew anything about—*BANG!*—Second Corinthians 4:7: 'But we have this treasure in jars of clay . . .'"

"Marshal Wilton!" Fessup began jumping around. "That verse is talkin' about the gospel—"

Marshal Wilton brought a heavy hand down on his deputy's shoulder. "Listen to me, Fessup. Don't you see what's going on out there? I always had a sneakin' suspicion Wade Bookman had a better grip on his cards than his Bible. This just proves it!"

"But why aren't they catchin' on to each other's misfires?"

"It's hard for a man to know what's wrong if he doesn't know what's right, Fessup."

"All right, Page," Wade Bookman's voice rang out. "So you know where old miners stash their gold nuggets. But I'm takin' you to the limit this time."

"Whatcha reckon Bookman's up to, Marshal?" Parley asked.

"I don't know. But something tells me this'll be the last shot for both men."

"You listenin', Page?" Bookman shouted.

"I hear ya."

"You get this one, and I'll ride outta town. You miss it, and *you're* history around here. Deal?"

A gust of wind banged a shutter against a building. Finally Page spoke. "Deal, Bookman."

"All right, then. I'll give you to the count of 10. What's your fancy black book have to say about what *real* Scripture slingers oughta eat? If you're the 'real' thing, you'll know how to chow down like it. *Right*, Page? Now, go! One, two . . ."

A cold sweat broke out on Turner Page's brow. He'd never heard about a special diet for Scripture slingers before. He tore through his Bible like a tornado in a Kansas wheat field.

"Five, six . . ." The sound of Bookman's counting fogged his mind.

"Eight . . ." A panicky feeling swept over the desperate Scripture-slinger.

"Nine . . ."

"I've got it!" Page cried out. "Milk and honey! It's right here in—"

"Forget it, Page!" Bookman leaped out from behind the rain barrel. "I've got *you!*"

The other man rose cautiously from behind the water trough. "What are you talkin' about?"

"I'm callin' your bluff, Page. If you were a true-blue Scripture slinger you'd know I had no right to call another 'slinger's eatin' habits into question." *BANG!* "Colossians 2:16: 'Therefore do not let anyone judge you by what you eat or drink . . .'"

"Marshal!" Fessup cried, "that verse ain't talkin' about Scripture slingers' eatin' habits! It's about some early Christian—" Fessup's voice was suddenly drowned out by the roar of Turner Page's wrath.

"Why, you dirty river rat. You tricked me!"

"I played by the rules, Page," Bookman yelled back.

"Well, maybe I'll just take those rules and—"

"Hold it right there!" Both men turned in surprise toward the sound of Marshal Wilton's voice.

Bookman took a step backward. "Oh, now you stay out of this, Marshal," he warned as the lawman approached.

"That's right," Page added. "This is between Bookman and me."

"And I'm comin' between *both* of you," Marshal Wilton said firmly. "I've been listenin' to you two Bible bashers do more damage to the Scriptures than a buckin' bronco to a greenhorn, and I've had all of it I can stand."

"What're you drivin' at?" Page asked.

The marshal reached over and took the man's Bible and opened it. "Listen up real good now, both of you. See if this here verse triggers anything: 'Do your best to present yourself to God as one approved, a workman who does not need to be ashamed *and who correctly handles the word of truth.*'" The marshal paused, then looked up and added, "Second Timothy 2:15."

The two Scripture slingers stared at each other, then turned back toward the marshal.

"Gentlemen," Marshal Wilton continued as he gently closed the book, "the next stage out of town leaves at 6:00. I hope you *both* have a nice trip. Oh, and here's something to read along the way." The marshal handed Page's Bible back to him and walked away.

* * *

Wade Bookman's moustache twitched slightly as he and Turner Page played another game of "Scripture Fours" on the eastbound stage.

And that same night, quite a few folks around town started reading the Bible *for themselves*.

THE WINK BLINKMAN SHOW

by Bill Cleveland

A*pplause sign on]*

Thank you. Yes. What an audience! Thank you . . .

[Applause sign off; audience settles down]

Welcome to our show, ladies and gentlemen. I'm your host, Wink Blinkman, and what a show we have for you today. People are still buzzing over the social event of the . . . well, of all time! And we have an exclusive for you. Our guests today are the five young ladies who were invited to the wedding and were all dressed up in their gowns and were there—but somehow didn't get in! Yes, that's right! *They didn't get in!*

[Oohs, aahs]

Yes, ladies and gentlemen, here they are, all five, right here on our stage! Let's give them a big hand.

[Applause]

Today they are going to tell us, in their own words, just what went wrong on that momentous night. Ladies, thank you for coming. I know this is very difficult, especially since it's been just hours since you missed the event of a lifetime. We'll be asking you some questions, but first, some messages from our sponsors.

[Lots of boring commercials]

Welcome back. Shirley Q is the top student in her junior high class. She has studied all about the Bridegroom and His coming marriage. Last month she turned in a paper in which she expressed doubts that the wedding would take place as soon as everyone thought it would—even if it would take place at all! Shirley, how are you feeling this morning? . . .

Disappointed? Well, I can certainly understand that. I believe you consider yourself kind of an expert on the signs that showed the wedding was near—you know, the wars, earthquakes, signs in the heavens. How could a sharp kid like you not be ready? . . .

Well, yes, there are wars all the time. Yes, it certainly does seem that disasters are always hitting somewhere . . . Just a meteor shower and a solar eclipse? Well, I suppose you might have been on firm *scientific* ground in thinking that the wedding wouldn't be for many years, if at all. But don't you think there are things that science can't explain and that we must have faith—

OK, I see where you're coming from. Well, Shirley, if it is any consolation to you, I heard that some of the most educated people of the community missed out also.

You all know Mavis R. She's the first young lady to be elected president of the student body, president of the student senate, and chairperson of the local chapter of the Young Republicans. She has her eye on becoming the first woman governor of our state and then . . . the White House! Why not? Mavis, as a budding young politician, how could you have missed such an important function? . . .

You had some meetings to attend . . . a key vote . . . Oh, you don't think the Bridegroom understands politics? Why do you say that? . . .

Yes, He certainly did have a chance just to waltz on in to the highest office in Judea, take over the government, and teach those awful Romans a lesson. Oh, and then set about making this a world where people can live together in peace and prosperity.

Well, Mavis, those are admirable goals, but that doesn't seem to have been the Bridegroom's plan. So you have decided to work inside the system, something He wasn't willing to do. Well, we all hope you are able to make this world the utopian society you want, but I don't know . . .

OK, everybody welcome Allison F!

[Applause]

Allison F is well known as one of this area's leading young sports figures. A future Olympian, many say, whose list of accomplishments is truly dazzling. Starred in junior high track, lettered in basketball, ace pitcher for the Lavender Sox softball team—Allison, pardon me for putting it like this, but you really struck out on this one . . .

Yes, we know that you've always "gone for the gold," and you certainly do "win some and lose some." And your motto is "Just do it." But tell me, you are known as a hard worker, sometimes squeezing out extra time on the practice field from schoolwork, your family, and, well, even your spiritual life. It seems you are always either doing laps or in the gym pumping iron. Were you really properly prepared for this event? . . .

Right, I guess you weren't "focused" last night . . . You are really going to be "up" for the next wedding? Well, I'm sorry to have to be the one to tell you, but there isn't going to be a rematch on this one. That was the super bowl of weddings, the world series of social events. Sorry . . .

Hold on to your hats, ladies and gentlemen; here she is, Lavern P!

[Loud applause]

Lavern P, star of the hit TV series *26007*, is currently one of America's most "in" teens. She admits she didn't know too much about the Bridegroom before—you know, she's kind of gone Hollywood, Tinseltown—but when she got the invitation, she decided to make a fashion statement that would "burn up the tabloids!" Lavern darling, why don't you tell us all about it . . .

White stretch limo, sure! Entourage of 12, of course! An Oscar de la Renta original? Wow, that's really hot! But what about the gown the Bridegroom provided for everyone to wear? . . .

Well, sure, it wasn't too bad for "off the rack," and yes, you certainly do have a rep to live up to . . . You alerted the press and your fans so they could be there to see your entrance? You were interviewed by Barry Art of *Lifestyles of the Fabulously Wealthy and Extremely Cool?* Well, of course you had to sign autographs . . . Oh, and by the time you were ready to make your grand entrance, the ceremony was almost over. Well, sure, everybody knows celebrities are usually late, and I guess you *were* kind of miffed at them for locking the door on you, but hey, that's show business! . . .

[Applause]

Finally, we have with us Sally T, just your ordinary garden-variety churchgoing teenager. Welcome, Sally! How does it feel to be in such distinguished company? . . . Really an honor, you say, if it weren't under such sad circumstances? I can imagine how you feel, especially since you have been one of the Bridegroom's most faithful boosters . . . You don't really know what happened—you just got busy? Busy doing what, if I may ask? . . .

Right, you were putting the finishing touches on your Sabbath school program . . . a stint on the Community Services van . . . Wow, three hours with the Pathfinders at their car wash to raise money for new uniforms! Say, when do you even have a chance to breathe? . . . More? Little Sisters, the teen interfaith dinner at Ralston's Restaurant . . . Kind of just slipped up on you, huh? Didn't your pastor preach a series on the coming wedding? . . .

Oh, you were ushering, collecting the offering, helping out with the little kids . . . You missed *all* the sermons? Well, I can certainly sympathize . . .

Oh, and there was something even worse? The Bridegroom said He didn't even know you? There, there, somebody hand her a tissue. Well, ladies and gentlemen, when we come back from station break we are going to have an exclusive Wink Blinkman flashback!

[Boring commercials]

We're back.

[Applause: tape of past show rolls on the monitor]

We are talking to the noted religious author Matthew, who's just written a best-seller on the life and times of the Messiah. He's been sharing with us a number of interesting and inspirational things from his biography of Jesus, the coming Bridegroom. Matt, I understand there are some very startling things in chapter 24, and we don't want to let you get away without sharing them with us . . .

Oh, so you think that a few excerpts might just kind of speak for themselves? OK.

[Reads Matthew 24:3-14]

Truly astonishing, Matt, truly astonishing! I was moved—and shaken! It's so plain. I don't see how anyone who reads these words can possibly miss this great event! . . . A lot of people will? . . . Perhaps some right here in this audience? Well, I hope not! That really would be a shame!

That's it, ladies and gentlemen. If you would like an original transcript of this program, please write to us in care of this station. See you next week!

[Applause; credits roll]

HAPPY SABBATH, THOMPSONS!

by Maylan Schurch

CHAD, DO I have to come in there and—?"

"*No!*"

"Then get up!"

"I *will*, Mom."

"The bathroom's free. Sandy's out. But I've got to do my hair in 15 minutes."

"OK."

"Chad?"

"*OK!*"

* * *

My Sabbath sunband curves slowly around My planet, washing holy delight across the land. Happy Sabbath, Thompsons.

* * *

"Chad?"

"Don't come in, Sandy."

"My hair curler's by the sink. Hand it out."

"I can't."

"I *need* it, Chad. *Mom!*"

"Just shut up and give me a minute . . . There. Take your stupid—"

"Mom! Mom! He burned me on the arm!"

"I didn't mean to!"

* * *

To My 74 dying children in Karachi I will give a vision of heaven as they fall asleep. For My children in the Thompson home I will arrange for two squirrels and a crow to have a friendly fight in their front yard. This will give them something to talk about in the car on the way to church.

* * *

"Look at that squirrel, Chad. Sandy, look!"

"There's two of them, Mom. What are they doing?"

"Chad, don't throw rocks at them. They're all right. I think they're just playing."

"Mom, look! That crow's after them."

"We'd better go. Come on, kids. Into the car."

"I feel sick."

"Chad, I said get into the car."

"No, Mom, I feel really sick. I want to stay home."

"Get in the car! That's better."

"Mom?"

"Oh, Sandy, now what?"

"I forgot my Bible."

"Here, take the keys. Get it. *Quick!* Chad, do you have yours?"

"No."

"Sandy! Get Chad's, too. Chad, you should always bring your Bible. Don't you get points when you have your Bible?"

"Nahhhhh."

* * *

So much for the Sabbath nature. Happy Sabbath, Thompsons. Be glad you aren't living in Cambodia. Most of My children in Cambodia didn't have a breakfast like yours. Most of them don't have cars to ride in. What they do have is guerrilla warfare. That's why they have such happy Sabbaths—it reminds them of heaven.

* * *

"Psst, psst, pssst."

"Sandy, could you look up Deuteronomy 8:18? Please, Sandy? Now, the rest of you girls please keep quiet."

"Psst, psst, pssst."

"Girls!"

"Deuteronomy *what?*"

"Eight eighteen, Sandy. Read it loud and clear."

" 'But thou shalt—' "

"Psst, psst, psst."

"Girls, please!"

" '—thou shalt remember the Lord thy God . . .' "

* * *

I am angry with two men in Bogota who are driving a dynamite-loaded truck to the door of a shopping center. It will not go well with them on the last day. When they see then the full horror of what they are about to do, when the pain and blood and child-screaming really surround their senses, then they will cry out for death themselves.

I am coming back. And then we will have real Sabbath rest at last.

* * *

"Our closing song is number 432, 'Shall We Gather at the River.' Let's stand."

"Hey, Sandy, let's sing the wrong verse. Let's do verse 3."

"Three?"

"Yeah. *'Ere we reach the sinning river . . .'*"

"Chad! Sandy!"

"What?"

"Sing the song right."

"What, Mom?"

"You heard me."

"What?"

"Do you want me to take you outside? Right now?"

"What?"

* * *

What the Thompsons need is six months in Peru. That's really all it would take, just six months. Out there on Lake Titicaca, going to school with My dirt-poor children in the floating villages, baby-sitting, tutoring children, teaching English. The only problem would be getting them to come back home. They'd want to stay. There's so much to do.

* * *

"Mom?"

"What?"

"Can I go on a bike ride?"

"Finish your food, Chad."

"It is finished."

"No, it's not. Finish it."

"OK, but then can I go on a bike ride?"

"Where to?"

"Oh, just around."

"Mom, he's going to go down to the mall and watch the video games. On *Sabbath*."

"No, I'm *not*, Sandy, you airhead!"

"Yes, he is, Mom. He goes down there and watches them."

"Sandy, that's enough. Chad, you stay here this afternoon."

"Mom!"

* * *

Come, come, Thompsons. Why don't you go visit Cherry, the girl with cerebral palsy who can't come to church? A half hour's chat with her would make her whole month. Why don't you invite that migrant family to go to the park with you this afternoon? And of course, there's the nursing home with all those precious, wise, weary children of Mine.

Happy Sabbath, Thompsons. Don't have one—make one.

KEEP THE STORIES COMING!

To enjoy great *Guide*® stories and faith-building activities each week, simply fill out and mail the form below!